The Gasconade Review presents:
Ladies' Night

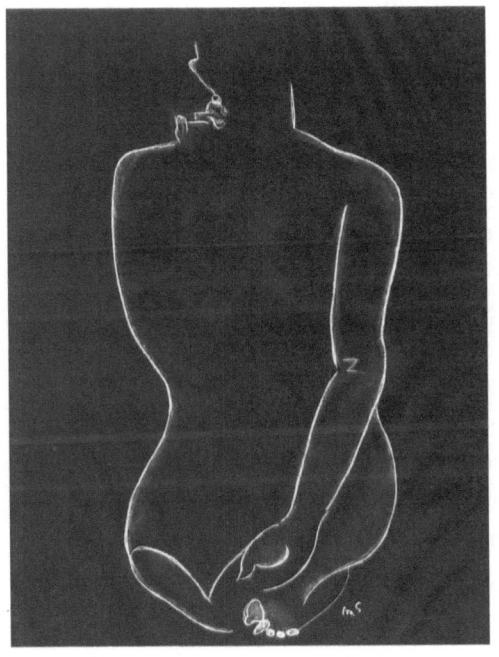

Edited by Rebecca Weber, John Dorsey
and Jason Ryberg

Spartan Press
Kansas City, MO
spartanpresskc@gmail.com

OAC Books
Belle, MO
www.osageac.org

Copyright © Jason Ryberg, 2019
First Edition 1 3 5 7 9 10 8 6 4 2
ISBN: 978-1-950380-68-8
LCCN: 2019954002

Design, edits and layout: Jason Ryberg, John Dorsey
Title page image: Diminuendo II by Marcy Smalley
All rights reserved. No part of this publication may be reproduced or transmitted in any form or by any means, electronic or mechanical, including photocopying, recording or by info retrieval system, without prior written permission from the author.

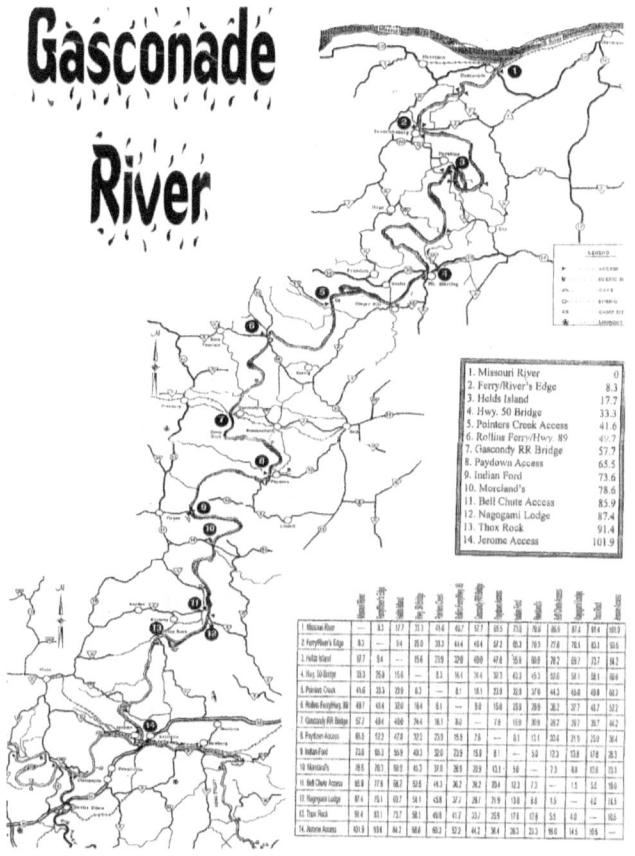

The **Gasconade River** is about 280 miles (450 km) long and is located in central and south-central Missouri in the United States. The Gasconade River begins in the Ozarks southeast of Hartville in Wright County and flows generally north-northeastwardly through Wright, Laclede, Pulaski, Phelps, Maries, Osage and Gasconade counties, through portions of the Mark Twain National Forest. It flows into the Missouri River near the town of Gasconade in Gasconade County.

The name Gasconade is derived from "Gascon", an inhabitant of the French region of Gascony. The people of that province were noted for their boastfulness. It was applied by the early French to the Indians living on its banks who bragged about their exploits. The name means to boast or brag, and thus the river received its name. The waters of the river are boisterous and boastful and the name is also descriptive.

The headwaters of the Gasconade are in the southeastern corner of Webster County northeast of Seymour, Missouri where it drains the eastern margin of the Springfield Plateau at approximately 37°11'54"N 92°41'44"W. The river joins the Missouri River at the city of Gasconade at 38°40'28"N 91°32'55"W The river follows a meandering course through the Ordovician age dolostone and sandstone bedrock of the Ozark Salem Plateau creating spectacular bluffs and incised meanders along the way. Numerous springs and caves occur within the drainage area and along the river course. Significant tributaries include the Osage Fork of Webster and Laclede counties and Roubidoux Creek and Big Piney River of Texas and Pulaski counties. The Roubidoux and Big Piney flow respectively along the west and east boundaries of Fort Leonard Wood which lies a short distance south and east of the Gasconade.

The plateau surface near the midpoint is 300 feet (91 metres) above the river bottom near the river midpoint northeast of Waynesville creating scenic river bluffs. At the junction with the Missouri the river bottom is about 400 feet (120 m) lower in elevation than the old plateau surface above the river. The elevation of the plateau rim at the headwaters is at or above 1,600 feet (490 m) with local hilltops at over 1,700 feet (520 m) (second highest elevation in Missouri near Cedar Gap). The elevation at the confluence with the Missouri is 500 feet (150 m) giving an overall drainage basin relief of 1,200 feet (370 m).

It is ranked with a difficulty of I and II (seldom) by those who canoe, kayak and float. It is considered a good float stream because there's typically not a heavy congestion of boats. It is common to go for many miles without seeing another boat.

There are caves and an abundance of wildlife along the river and is considered a popular place by anglers for its largemouth bass and smallmouth bass.

The Gasconade River is the longest river completely within the boundary of Missouri. It has been called one of the world's crookedest rivers.

The **Gasconade Review** is a literary and arts publication based out of the Osage Arts Community (http://osageac.org/), located on the Gasconade River, just outside of Belle, Missouri. It appears twice annually, focusing primarily, but not exclusively, on writers and artists from the region and state, but occasionally also features *folks what ain't from around here*. All submissions must be hand delivered between the months of April and October and the hours of 3pm to 6pm. A decent bourbon is appreciated. Proper river attire required. Don't worry, the dogs won't bite.

The Gasconade Review was created as part of Belle's Poet Laureate project at the beginning of 2017. Originally founded as a means to showcase work by poets and artists from around the fine state of Missouri, our scope has since grown to include pieces from all over the American Midwest, and we're darn proud to be able to offer you the works in the volume you're currently holding in your hands.

—John Dorsey, Founding Co-Editor and first Poet Laureate of Belle, 2017-2019

TABLE OF CONTENTS

Restoration by Penny Thieme

LAURA MARTIN

Fat Women Shouldn't Wear Their Hair Long Because
   It Makes Them Look Like Mama Cass / 1
The End of Warm Days / 3
The Long Lost 11.5" Icons of
   Back-of-the-Closet Fashion / 4

RIKKI SANTER

Faye Takes a Breath / 5
Betty Boop Marries Herself / 7
Woman Painting Women / 9

PUMA PERL

The Taste of Rebellion / 12
Without Snow / 15
Jane Ormerod's Basement / 18

APRIL PAMETICKY

Coyote / 20
Today she is vicarious pregnancy ills / 21
Blur / 22

A.SUMMER JAVADI

If Guns Were Made Of Crayons / 23
Molasses Rewind: The Parable of the Pomegranate / 24
The Nuclear Family Blew Up! / 25

KAREN LILLIS

Joan's Birds / 27
Poem for Renée / 29
Kathy's Street / 31

JONIE MCINTIRE

Passage of the Divine Bird, Print on my
    Therapist's Wall / 34
Grand Island, NE / 36
Walker Red / 37

RYKI ZUCKERMAN

tyrannosaurus rex / 38
on his wall / 39
epsilon eridani / 40

BEVERLY ZEIMER

Footprints, Bottomland, and Old River Turtles / 42
Quarry Lake / 44
Black Sheep / 46

CLAUDIA BIERSCHENK

In Tray, Out Tray / 47
My father teaches me about the Iron Curtain / 48
The First American / 49

NIKKI ALLEN

baby teeth / 53
open plan / 54
ode to ferric oxide / 55

SANDRA FEEN

Youngest Bird / 56
Flight / 58
Middle Age Fit / 60

ROBIN FREELAND

Closure / 62
Methusaline's Long Lost Loves / 63
Released / 65

WENDY RAINEY

Girlie Show / 66
Distraction / 67
Comfort Pet / 69

TRINA DROTAR

Hart Island / 70
Cutting / 71
The Blue Shirt / 74

JYL ANAIS

No Trespassing / 76
Empty/ Rising Tide / 78
re(member) / 80

LAUREN SCHARHAG

The Macaws / 81
Epigenetics / 83
Inheritance / 85

MAUREEN SHERBONDY

The Bridge Crossing / 86

K.R. MORRISON

Lady Viking / 91
Life Letter to Anne Sexton / 93
Witch Poet / 95

HEATHER SULLIVAN

Cavern / 97
Where Wisdom Comes From / 98
Mama Loves You / 99

ELLARAINE LOCKIE

Sexed on a Kona Balcony / 100
Should Have Been a Boy / 102
Taking Issue with Marcelino / 104

AGNES VOJTA

Peace of the River / 106
We, the Argonauts / 107
Alea Iacta Est / 108

BARBARA MARIE MINNEY

Real Woman / 109
The Ornament / 110
Kintsugi / 111

D.C. BUSCHMANN

Gossip / 112
Nature's Irony / 113
Nature's Medicine / 114

PEGARTY LONG

Elvis! / 115

LORETTA DIANE WALKER

Why I Am Jealous of Princess Diana of Themyscira,
    Aka Wonder Woman / 119
Waiting with a Stranger / 121
Why I Can't Keep a Lover / 123

STEPHANIE BRYANT ANDERSON

Cliff Tracks | Train Babies [I Always Wanted to Write
    a Poem About A Train] / 124
Of Radishes or Wounds / 126
Here I Stand Horse Cropping Past / 127

NANCY P. DAVENPORT

Name-Calling Lasts Forever / 129
Eclipse Indifference / 131
Sonora Pocket Poem #1 / 133

DIANNE BORSENIK

Fahrenheit / 134
All That Jazz / 136
When the Son of a Motherless Goat
   Tries to Stare You Down, / 137

BARONESS VON SMITH

Club Wasteland / 138

ALEXIS RHONE FANCHER

this small rain / 140
June Fairchild isn't dead / 142
Poem For The Girl Who Wanted To Stop Time / 144

MICHELLE STORER

I found a letter you wrote / 146
The wind blew / 147
She won't let him / 148

KYLE LAWS

Autobiography of a Pearl / 149
Woman With Pearls / 151
Wilmington Stop / 152

FRANCINE WITTE

Breakthrough / 153
Any Other Street / 154
Daylights / 156

TRINA STOLEC

Scarred for Life / 158
Mountain Graveyard / 159
Nostalgia / 161

VICTORIA STERLING

Complex / 167
She is Beautiful / 169
What Lies Ahead / 170

HOLLY DAY

The Soldier / 171
Dying on a Monday / 172
Talking it Out / 173

CARRIE GREENLAW

Goddamn Hurricane / 174
Big Bang / 177
The Summer Room / 178

LINDA LERNER

When Death Is a Red Balloon / 180
Keeping Time / 182
Like A Prayer / 183

TOBI ALFIER

High Tea / 184
The Scent of New-Mown Wildflowers / 186
Hymn of the Farmer's Daughter / 188

DAWN CLAYTON

The Key / 190
Dirty Kids / 191
Where Does He Go? / 192

DENISE TERRIAH

Good Boy / 193

TERESA COSTA

Summer Queen / 199
Glowed In The Dark / 200
With Black Elk / 201

The Players / 202

Sensitvity to Initial Conditions by Penny Thieme

Sensitivity to Original Condition by Penny Theime

LAURA MARTIN

Fat Women Shouldn't Wear Their Hair Long
Because It Makes Them Look Like Mama Cass

My mom lied to me
and said Mama Cass
choked to death on a ham sandwich.
I hated the way she said it—
so matter-of-factly
taking a long drag on a Marlboro
watching nighttime soaps
dirty dinner dishes in the sink
and lunch dishes
and breakfast dishes
and random dishes from the day before
her hair in bristle curlers
her butt planted in her La-Z-Boy rocker for the evening,
she said it like she was there
or heard it from some grand authority
with giddy excitement like it just happened last week—
You know, she wasn't married ...
she made sure to point that out.

My mom lied to me
and said Mama Cass
choked to death on a ham sandwich,
but at least she didn't make that up—
she just read it in a rag paper and passed it along.

I'm sure every single bit of it
made sense to her though,
I'm sure she thought it true as truth itself:
a fat woman with a fat voice
coming out of her big fat mouth—
of course she died while shoving it all in,
of course she died in her bedroom alone.

The End of Warm Days

It's almost over now,
the watermelon having vined
but never bloomed,
the corn stalks having grown
only yay-high to the knees
kernel-less and stringy,
the rows of dried, outstretched
crooked sticks of failed tomato
standing united like forgotten scarecrows
in the blamed ground

Only what grew beneath survived—
the bright blushing radish
the sweet fat-fingered carrot
the shiny green onion
that stretched up to the sun and taunted
eat me eat me eat me from head to toe—
all begging to be released
from the cool watered earth,
and the shallow-buried offerings
of trout guts and catfish heads

From blossom to blight
this was always their way—
before the dirt ever first was broken
before the first seed even dropped
before the eager, impatient pull
of those first hungry hands.

The Long Lost 11.5" Icons of Back-of-the-Closet Fashion

I sewed my own doll clothes by hand
with stitches my father taught me—
cut up shirts I didn't like
and made sundresses for my Barbies.

Burgundy and green striped polyester sleeves
with circulation-cutting elastic at the wrist
sliced nicely in half long ways,
scissors gliding smooth along the seam.

Stitched tight across the bust of a plastic beauty,
the dress became all the rage that summer of '79
around the roasting pan pool
on the front porch step.

RIKKI SANTER

Faye Takes a Breath

Launched from the lake's muzzle
    your bones swirl
in amniotic womanhood
    against the undertow of adolescence.

Your face a full moon & you take
    breath, exhale flocks of dragonflies
& golden tadpoles, swallow
    old stories, deep song.

In time you will claim río debajo del rio
    your river beneath the river—
your hair blonde kelp, no life
    jacket or bow line

you are nimble,
    a vernal shapeshifter
treading waters
    of kith & kin.

Necklaces ripple 'round you,
    your sultry appointments with the world
may embrace fluidity—a she, a he,
    a them, *each to each.* You raise

your arms above your head
        then submerge—
Anaïs Nin tattooed onto each wrist,
        gift from your mother:

on left— *I must be a mermaid,*
        on right—*I have no fear of depths*
and a great fear
        of shallow living.

Betty Boop Marries Herself

Her camel kneels
& Betty steps down
into the midnight Ganges
feels the gentle push
of the current
when she submerges
the pearl halo of
her linen robe tiptoes
into the swirls
and eddies
of the river's open
throat. Her voice
lightly bebops
the waters to sleep.
She feels the barge
of napping monkeys
make safe passage
from her *vagina
dentata*. Calla lily
behind her ear
she launches
into the darkness
a leaf bowl
filled with
frangipanis,
her carved love
spoon a confident

oar. Betty's curves
dissolve into the tender
pull of current, red
petals bobbing
to the surface
like a menstrual
milky way.

Woman Painting Women

Let us not forget the horror that accompanies
the wonder; the horror of this story...
          —Marie Darrieussecq *Being Here is Everything:*
               The Life of Paula Modersohn-Becker (1876-1907)

Those who recall me claimed
Paula puzzled Paula—
suspicious of childbirth, flirtatious
with a bell-tower's dangling rope,
impatient with cooking classes,
miserable veal roast.

Copper kettle of long thick hair,
my commanding gait
through the moorlands of Worpswede.
My painter husband rubbed pristine
bark and leaves between his fingers.
I, with chalk and charcoal, limned
dignity into what was gnarled—
peasants bound to the soil
sunken women weathered
and work-worn, their thick
hands like spades, tidy
mouths in tangles of thought—
and little girls forever sequestered
from womanhood
but pensive just the same—
my sisterhood in foxgloves,

hollyhocks, marigolds,
my ancestry in lemons,
apples, amber.

Paris was my wildfire contagion
asparagus and melon at the bistros,
thunderstorms of invention
brewing in the galleries.
Rilke liked my studio filled with lilies.
I liked my studio red-striped
in between testaments of turquoise
and navy blue.

But it was my nudity
in self-portrait,
barometer of my becoming,
each portrait my private

cave wall, each brushstroke
trailing particles
of voluptuous gaze
from me in back silver.

Skulled fiddler at my bedside
the last weeks of my life,
baby daughter at my breast
while I exhaled Cezanne,
inhaled Gauguin, the staircase

they illuminated for me.
Who can ever take credit
for doing something first.
A pity my last-breath
pact between art and sorrow
between nascent soul
and shadow dancer.

PUMA PERL

The Taste of Rebellion

What did your rebellion taste like?
Mine tasted like long-haired boys
Sounded like 4AM rock and roll,
felt like the bottom
of my mother's staircase
after she kicked me out
for coming home too late

My rebellion tasted of not going back,
smelled like $34 in my wallet,
dug into me like the knife
resting in a sheath on my hip
the day I changed my name
to Puma, just like my knife

My rebellion felt like never going home,
feelings began in my legs,
exploded like the orgasms
I'd never even had yet,
smelled like pot and silk scarves
burning shade on lightbulbs,
looked like paisley,
reds and blues melting
on purple
Sounded like Jimi and Janis
before they reached 27
and draped the Fillmore in black

Nobody witnessed my rebellion,
everybody caught up in their own
My family had already labelled me
crazy, hopeless, a lost cause,
a loser nobody would love
They were wrong and they were right

His rebellion was dropping out
of Bronx Science, hiding a gun
in his bureau, black jeans so tight
he *customized* them
with slits up the calf
and could hardly walk up the five flights
leading to our railroad apartment
with the police lock, the brick wall,
the loft bed, the bathtub in the kitchen
Where we lived in our shared rebellion

Our rebellion was his criminality,
my welfare, our books and music,
the dog he called Stagger Lee,
nights in Tompkins Square Park
days on St. Mark's Place,
armed love, cigarettes
leather jackets

My surrender was to heroin,
His was to money
A baby born in the middle
of the surrender

His rebellion would be raves,
speed, cars, girls, and survival

The drugs are gone
Stagger Lee was stolen
from outside a bodega
and his owner's life surrendered
to the gun held in his own hand

My rebellion is quiet and solitary
Broken down Tuesdays
and hot summer days when life
seems to go on too long

Today is Wednesday, July 4th
Fireworks but no celebration
I order Chinese food and search
for a black and white movie
If new Coltrane tracks can be found
Maybe there's still some hope
for rebellion without surrender.

Without Snow

Are you lonely?
I don't understand
the question.
Or why you asked.
I don't even know the answer.
If I did, I'd never admit it.
Not to you.

It's like asking tropical islanders
if they like snow.
Maybe they are missing something,
without snow.
But how could they know?

I don't speak
the *we* language.
I eat
all the chicken legs
and sleep
diagonally
across the bed.

When I was a kid,
my father ate
the chicken legs.
I cried
and my mother yelled at him.

He left the table and closed
the bedroom door,
fell asleep
on top of the blankets.
Stayed on his side
of the bed.

I started eating my meals alone.
It doesn't matter
if I eat a baked potato.
Or a steak.
Or not at all.

You withdraw the question.
There is no good answer.
Yes implies need.
No implies rejection.
I say nothing.
Silence is an art.
Or a weapon.

It's Easter Sunday.
Last night,
I forgot to look
for the last blue moon.

There are ten eggs,
one apple, one orange,
and a Dixie cup size
ice cream container
in my refrigerator.

Caramel cone.
The refrigerator
looks lonely.
I live.
Without snow.

Jane Ormerod's Basement*

You can't love your child because nobody loved you
You hate the Bronx because you got mugged in Brooklyn
You're afraid to get a dog because they killed your cat

It's what happened in the attic
It's what happened in the basement

Years pass
Nothing matters, everything counts

Love
Loss
Life

What else is left besides fear?

Sobriety's irrelevant if you don't want to drink
Success is compromised when everything runs smoothly
Love only happens when the garbage is taken out
Loss is another way of saying Wednesday
And life, as usual, doesn't care

There are stoops on East 10th Street
We sit in a sliver of sun, talk about Monk and Coltrane,
Coney Island and the poems we wrote and didn't write,
the first books we bought, HOWL and Ferlinghetti,
the people we miss, lives lost in the thick air,

indecision and a cup of coffee, club soda and a car,
we circle and return to certainty and all that matters

Love, Loss, Life and what else is left besides fear?
Could be a book title, don't ya think?

Poet Jane Ormerod wrote one of the best lines I've ever read: "We refuse to enter the basement because of something that happened in the attic," from "Belongings (Must Dress the Character").

APRIL PAMETICKY

Coyote

For a while we're lying in the divets our bodies and time
    have created
on our parallel sides of the mattress.

I can hear the weighted stillness from your side of the bed,
the measured breath,
awful effort to pretend to sleep.

You stir at the sound of the train a quarter-mile down the road,
horn calling out to warn travelers from crossing over,

And then the coyotes call,
subtle yippling and laughter,
echo back to the train from the pack denning
on the eastern shore of our subdivision pond.

You move closer,
over the geographic divide of hummock and down comforter,
curl me into your space.
We hold and listen to the howls,
the crisp night broken by song.

Today she is vicarious pregnancy ills

Today she is vicarious pregnancy ills,
shadowy remembrance of fetid bloat,
swollen toes,
ghost of rib kicks
and gas bubbles.

Today she is tides of wheat,
whipping stalks bowed down in
waves by stepbrother wind.

She is plastic ring from milk jug,
hard-boiled eggs at breakfast,
smell of dryer lint and charcoal flame,
empty womb a round echoing drum.

She will float on wood floors,
creak with weight and bad knees crackling,
sit in the hum of air conditioning and preservatives.

Blur

Today she is endless lists,
sleepless nights,
barometric pressure
too hot
then too cold
shallow breaths around lump in chest.

She reaches for toes but settles for knees.
She is egg baskets and shredded plastic,
chocolate she won't eat
as long as it isn't in her house

When she was a child in PE,
her stomach was called the breadbasket.
where soul resides,
Just beneath the breastbone still a little bruised,
All the way down to pelvic tilt,
guts
innards
and chakras.
She is gulp and swallow
tired eyes,
blurry.

A. SUMMER JAVADI

If Guns Were Made Of Crayons

There is no warmth in metallic silver,
That granite gray leaves dead brown babies,
On garbage filled streets.
This hexadecimal syndrome,
Stuffs fresh cut wax as trash bagged wallflowers,
Their petals wilted,
They would have colored white within the lines of clouds,
But rain dropped skies full of bullets,
Left their playgrounds empty.
Their shrill laughter,
Echoes off beautiful, tax dollar mosques.
Dancing baby angels play hopscotch near Crayola crayons,
No longer rolling from chilled, stubby fingers.
Do they build sandcastles in the East?
Or does the ocean of oil knock down those walls,
Pulled in, by the tides of the men,
Whose glasses of Merlot stain bloodthirsty teeth.
Is that the color of red we see,
As we open our fresh, cut crayons,
On our first days of school?
I reckon not... While they draw stick figures in the sands,
Americans draw constitutional guns in hand,
Wrapped in bloodshed red, dessert ghost white,
And flat-line, code blue.
And if guns were made of Crayons,
I doubt Humpty Dumpty's men,
Would care to color him in,
That white-washed hue.

Molasses Rewind: The Parable of the Pomegranate

The light transfers in this season;
10 minus 3,
Equaling a fast,
Bit by byte,
Incredibly loud reverb.
Suspended in Catschup, forget the fries,
Green tomatoes offer juice,
Physiologically unresponsive; noosed,
OH! -That noise.
This reality; with all her deceptions,
Is rallying a down shift,
Atomic compromise.
Forced shift-shaping of a Lycan tribe,
Slightly right, but not at all right,
Sinister; left trying to envelope the existence,
Leather binding, crafty; this cunning transMUTative silence,
Edging closer, to the chain-linked fence,
Peter rabbit has rabies; no, no babies;
Into nothing; or maybe all would prefer,
Such wholesomeness; I digress.

The Nuclear Family Blew Up!

The townspeople all had that same damn water mill design,
Burnt orange and prairie brown up on their couches,
I had a white letterman's sweater,
With a big, fat letter "A" plopped up on the front of it.
And the powder blue make-up,
I sure didn't laugh when the act was up,
So grew my disgust,
And the current number playing on the radio,
Calls the nerves.
Not by Honey, Sugar, or Miss;
But, by the indiscreet profanities,
Of a bronzed, wall-street call girl.
How could they sing along with this perverse dirge?
Such a vagrant flatter,
The hearse is here,
Before even the last Barr,
And the soda pop fountain of my youth,
Has all but dried up from here.
The reckless noise of a crazed navy brat,
Dances down the ploys,
Beaver Cleaver's screams from the bloody nightmare,
Under his bed is Wally's corpse.
He had strangled himself,
With the American Dream,
He couldn't take another sex filled scene.
Must have been one of those Ragheads,
Stealing his girl,

The bird took to the Middle East,
Like a dog in heat,
So fast--
Her feathers sizzled in the Valvoline.
He'll probably make her cover those curls,
That matched her tangled nest,
And the eggy splatter of nationalist pride,
Captured on his deceased, bloated, red face,
Nearly lost my pace,
Would have even the bees knees shutter
I guess the nuclear family blew up!

KAREN LILLIS

Joan's Birds

Our winter birds are back
If we can call them our birds
When Joan insists they're hers
Joan is older than the hills
Older than her brother Bill, who's
Already had his tongue cut out
And before that, the trach
Still he nags you to quit the smoking.
He writes it on a pad of paper he carries
In his shirt pocket.

Joan won't quit. Smoking hasn't killed her yet.
She tells you to defy her brother, do what you want.
She tells you that her birds are from McKees Rocks,
That the backyard slopes are full of windshield glass
Ground to gravel, that Art Junior hacked out all the
Rose bushes, one by one, just before we got here.
Joan smokes your old brand, Pall Mall unfiltereds.
In winter, she tries to pay you when you shovel
Her front walk. In the summer, she makes sure
You trim the grass so the drivers who speed past
Know the difference between the houses we inhabit
And the homes that were left behind, discarded.
Bill was supposed to die of the throat cancer, but
Then he didn't. What was left to do, except buy
That city-owned Victorian for five thousand,

The one he could see from his sister's couch,
That house that was relieved of its plumbing,
Its copper, its electric juice. Bill who was stationed
In Japan didn't mind at all, taught himself how to
Install pipes, install wires. Joan cooked him soups
While the blood returned to his veins. Bill who couldn't
Get enough of the *panpan* girls of Okinawa, he wrote
That for you on the pad of paper, too. You were coming
Home from a smoke walk, and the black birds were
Screaming and diving from one side of the road
To the other, from Joan's branches to Amir's and back
Again. You're not like Joan, you've quit the cigarettes
Twenty times in the ten years we've been nesting
Together. I'm not like you, I can't spend too long
In this hill town without catching a plane to the West
Coast, a train to the East. Bill always seems restless
When we see him, now that he's sided his house,
Glassed in the front porch, finished the trim
In a Wedgewood blue.

Poem for Renée

I was thinking about that fable.
The one about the scorpion and the frog.
How does it go?
Something about the scorpion, who
Bites the hand that feeds her,
Even though it brings death all around.
Something about a riverbank.
Something about drowning.

It's not to be confused with the one about
The scorpion who eats her own venom
And burns her own poems
For warmth
And starves her pleasures
And hides her light under a 9 to 5
And spends her worth fetching coffee and
Faxes and lunch platters and font sizes
For the fox and the turtle and the jackal and the frog.

Which is not to be confused either
With the scorpion who stings the frog on dry land
In a house
On high ground
And then runs so fast down Pig Hill
She burns her whole life behind her.

The life burns so bright
She has enough light to cross an ocean
At night.
She flies so far
She makes it all the way to Paradise.
She hunts so well
She finds a room
By the seashore.
Enough room for a poem desk
Enough poison to fill a pen
Enough pride to sting a line
Enough grief to line a widow's trousseau
With new sonnets
And new siren songs
And shark teeth bracelets

And amethyst amulets
And ancient fish-hooks
And new lunge poses
And new moon phases
And soothing sunsets
And healing garnets
And red hot hexes
And seaweed veils
And banshee wails
She can't help it
It's just
In her nature.

Kathy's Street

Meet me downtown
I'll get off work and we'll
go find the Revolution
Kathy Acker said it's waiting
for us on St. Mark's Place
oh, but that was 20 years ago
and a lot's changed since then
Kathy knows the street energy
it takes to make a Revolution
now all that concentration's departed
for points cyber
and under-river:
the hours spent on the internet
and cell phones
not to mention
interborough commuting trains
taking us farther and farther and farther
away

Nevermind
I'll meet you after work
we'll go looking for the last three
people who still get laid by meeting at cafes
in Manhattan
Oh, but I keep forgetting
I never leave work
I sleep and I dream work

I walk and I train work
I work work
I eat to keep the machine lean and healthy
so I can come home and work
after work
and why not?
Work is Freedom
War is Peace
and other epithets of
psychopathology I hoped we'd
leave behind us when we
left our Daddy's House: The 20th Century
I left daddy's house at age 18
for good it was
before I lost my virginity
but not before I was raped: oh
make no mistake
I was not *actually raped*
by my *actual father*
only a puny stand in
My actual father
loves me to pieces
and raised me thinking
I was an Indian
and my name was Scout
I was the leader of our hikes
except sometimes when I was Tree
and I'd meditate on what that meant
hoping someday I'd grow into
a fine old oak with branches strong

and the world would grow into
a new millennium that cared about the
color green (of leaves) and the
oxygen I would exhale

Oh but that, too was long
ago

Meet me downtown
the Revolution tonight
is in the blue cast of
twilight on sidewalk piles
of unlikely late-spring snow
outside Dojo's
Quick let's catch it
before it fades or melts
or both

(Previously published in the *LadyFest East Anthology, 2004* and
From Somewhere to Nowhere: The End of the American Dream, 2017)

Jonie McIntire

Passage of the Divine Bird, Print on my Therapist's Wall

From the leatherbound chair,
she asks me if I know
when anxiety will hit.

Says *trigger* like a horse
everyone has tamed,
like I have an emotional

class schedule – morning of ruminant
thoughts, lunch of abstract fears,
dinner with mourning - strict

and separated by bells.
She says perhaps,
if we pinpoint

when it starts, then we can get
ahead of it, can set our GPS
to the specifics

of my fear of failure, defensiveness,
and just redirect, redirect,
proceed to route.

On her wall, the bird scatters
itself in paint, each bit lifting off
the white canvas.

And in the chair, I squirm,
bits of my life blurted out
above her white carpet.

Grand Island, NE

The wind hisses
at the metal skin of our house,
throws knives so sharp
the dogs line themselves along
my legs, twitching as they dream.

Piled on us,
comforter, afghan, afghan
ripple over us like sandhills.

Under our blankets we are fresh sweat,
listening to Eric Clapton
slowhand as January throws its tantrum,
as fog hovers at power lines, frosts
the insides of windows.

We sleep and radiate.

Walker Red

Grandmas aren't
for comfort

not the ones
in the wood,

not the forest-edge
bright cloak gifts

who fight
quietly through

the beast's belly
while their women

children's children
skip into whispering

along paths
beaten smooth,

past whiskey wolves'
too long teeth

and big big eyes
waiting to pounce.

RYKI ZUCKERMAN

tyrannosaurus rex

why do they always show me
with my mouth open, snarling,
a mouth breather, vicious,
gleam in eye?
why do they make fun of my small upper arms,
whose petiteness balances my yin/yang?
it wounds me to be so maligned.
come closer and stroke my neck
to console me.
you look delicious.

on his wall

there is no creature shown
where his picture should be.
there is a far distant swamp,
the camera poised too high.

he can not get a leg up
and never smiles.
speech classes could not
correct his sibilance.

he left the garden so long ago
he has forgotten the smell of paradise,
still wary of apples and long-haired women.
the shape of vowels hurts his throat.

who is the friend of the snake?
that page is blank,
though there's a link
to hand-crafted cobra skin boots
with matching handbags.

epsilon eridani

for my late father, lover of sci-fi

astronomers sing of
its radiant moons,
a little like our earth.
future generations might build
their dream house there.

anywhere a mist might rise,
there grow amoebae.
anywhere a tear might fall,
dew lifting off leaves,
settling on the surface
of primordial slime.

a lunar place
circling a planet
twinkling among
the distant stars
so many set out for,
spun stories &
chanted in tongues about -

you might be there now:
still shaking your head
that the clothes you read about
in '30's sci fi novels —
the spacesuits of rigid plastic,

the futuristic styles
for intergalactic lolling around —
had actually arrived,
but fooled you,
as you pointed to your
polyester pants, your nylon scarf,
your acrylic sweater,
the soft side of plastic
for life on earth.

BEVERLY ZEIMER

Footprints, Bottomland, and Old River Turtles

Just outside South Bloomfield,
off Route 316,
the Scioto River
runs through the family farm.

I follow the riverbank,
catch sight of two pancake turtles
on the other side of the river—
one a good three feet wide,

the other a bit smaller—
basking in the sun.
I step softly on this bottomland,
a mile to the bridge.

My footsteps travel back in time,
take me to an ancient village.
I walk among arrowheads and stone axes
protected in Soil Bank.

Across the creaking iron bridge,
I hurry back
to the graveled spot where old turtles sun.
When they see me,

they stretch out long necks
and tilt pointed heads,
run to the water,
head for the muddy bottom.

Quarry Lake

It's Springtime at the quarry,
with late winter's clear, cold water
rippling a white boulder,
the Mallard's resting-place.

Ever mindful of his nearby flock,
he preens his emerald and chestnut feathers,
scans the blue surround,
scours his neck down

to his snowy breast.
Water plants, nuts, and seeds,
the sweet bark peel from white sycamore
lure this flock toward me.

Here they come webbing,
stocky bodies parting the water,
dipping, upending, tails fanning the scent
of the season's first rain.

They light upon a cluster of rocks,
shake lake from heads and tails,
stretch into the sky,
repeat the ritual of the drake's

scan and preen.
He sleeps to the hum of engines
as they descend Possum Run Road
brake, and accelerate Big Pansy Hill.

Gun fire cracks through the wood.
Iridescent purple and brown mottled feathers
flurry back into the water.
They paddle

to the bank on the other side,
leaving me with acorns,
and pebbles,
the sand between my toes.

Black Sheep

Praise to the black sheep!
Praise to her mother,
the wild ram, the scapegoat!

Praise to the Pickaway County farmer,
the hole in the fence
he forgot to mend!

Praise to the tall Sudan grass
where she hid,
missed the truck to the slaughterhouse!

She's the finest black sheep in Pickaway County.
Praise to the three bags full
they'll never get!

CLAUDIA BIERSCHENK

In Tray, Out Tray

In one tray,
jars of baby food,
apple sticks,
sore breasts.

In another tray,
rolled diapers,
scanned for their
contents.

And there is you,
on a weighing scales,
with a tape measure
and thermometer.

This is strange work.

My father teaches me about the Iron Curtain

It runs through us like a trench and
divides every day into decisions:
Here, there
staying, going.

The First American

I grew up in an East German village, close to the border with West Germany, where we never called anything by its name. The border was called *the Fence*. West Germany was referred to as *Over There*. If someone had managed to escape to the West, people would say, *they made it over* or *they got away*. If someone got arrested they had been "picked up".

Our world ended at the first checkpoint. That's where the border area began, which was called the *Zone* and the unfortunate inhabitants of the villages in the zone were commonly called *Zonies*. I say unfortunate, because these communities were almost completely isolated. The Zone was a bit like Willy Wonka's chocolate factory – nobody ever got in, nobody ever came out, unless you had a special permit issued by the People's Police.

Most of us had relatives in the West, who lived in pretty villages with half-timbered houses undarkened by a constant outpour of smoke and soot. I had seen them on TV and on colour photos relatives from *over there* passed around on their visits. I knew I would never see it for myself until I reached retirement age and would finally be allowed to travel. My West German relatives smelled crisp and fresh like the contents of the parcels they regularly sent us and which were always full of things unavailable in our country: real coffee, oranges, proper chocolate, cocoa, bed sheets (still in their packaging), and glossy colour magazines. They were not dressed in no-name-hand-me-downs like us, and the only economic advantage they had in visiting us was that they could fill up their cars with cheap petrol before crossing back over into their world.

If I stood on the tip of my toes stretching as far as I could from the attic window, I could catch a glimpse of the Fence snaking its way up the hillside through the forest in the distance. Somewhere over there people learned English instead of Russian. I enjoyed learning Russian, but I desperately wanted to learn English, mainly because I yearned to understand what Elvis Presley was singing about. His voice sounded the way custard tasted. When one of my mother's friends gave me an English textbook, I would sit in my room for hours and learn the whole book by heart. I would recite lists of words to everyone who was or wasn't interested, ignorant of any pronunciation rules: cat, can, car, paper, magazine, lorry. I showed off my knowledge at school and went even as far as claiming that I could now sing and translate the title song from *The Fall Guy*, a popular programme at the time, for those lucky enough to be able to tune into Western channels.

Then came the day when I would be able to put my linguistic achievements to practical use. An American was coming to the village! My father's cousin, who lived in Hannover, had married a real American, and they were coming for my Grandfather's birthday. It must have been 1985, when I was ten, or around that time. My mother had warned me not to spread the word too much at school, you never knew what consequences you'd have to bear when hosting a representative of the arch enemy. I couldn't care less and soon enough the whole village knew about it anyway. My father said it was no use making a big secret of it, because the men from *the Firm*, what the Secret Police was commonly referred to in East Germany, knew about our American entering the country even before *he* did. I wasn't concerned with any of that. I was concerned with the greeting I would extend to the American as soon as he'd walk through our door: *"I'm very pleased to meet **you**"*, *"I'm **very** pleased to meet you"* or rather *"I'm very **pleased** to meet you"*?

What would the American look like? I pictured him to be tall, muscular and blond, with white teeth, and a tattoo or two. In fact, my image of him faintly resembled this American actor my mother fancied, called Robert Redford. Surely he'd be chewing gum the whole time. If that was the case, I hoped he'd bring enough supplies, because the East German gum dissolved as soon as it hit your tongue. As the day of the arrival drew closer, I worked harder and harder on my English vocabulary: refrigerator, oven, forceps, hippopotamus. My only source, the English textbook, was soon covered in food stains and some pages were loosening, because I took it everywhere, even to the dinner table.

Grandfather's birthday was a Saturday, a sunny day in June, which meant I could be home from school before noon. (We had to go to school on Saturdays.) My mother had assured me the American would have already arrived by the time I got home. And sure enough, as soon as I turned the corner into our street, I saw THREE western cars parked outside our house - THREE! I could never tell a BMW from a Mercedes, but the difference between a sleek, shiny western car and our eastern *Trabant* was more than obvious. *The Trabant* resembled a plastic toy car and the staccato sound of its two-stroke engine could easily burst your eardrums.

I cannot remember how many people were crammed onto the sofa in Grandmother's *good* living room, which was only unlocked for Christmas, Easter, when the priest called, and for visitors from the West. There he was, looking lost in Grandfather's large beige armchair – the American! I was a bit disappointed. This American was short, thin, with black hair that was greying around the temples, big glasses, and very slim, perfectly manicured hands.

His teeth were large and yellow. I stood in front of him, stretched out my hand and said: *I'm very pleased to meet you!* He acknowledged my welcome with a smile and said something, which I didn't understand. It was the *first* time I heard someone talk English in *real time,* and it sounded like music! His name was Bob, short for Robert, and apart from being American he was also a Doctor.

During his two-day visit I followed Bob everywhere. I watched him eat, I watched him drink, I watched him talk or I just stood watching him as he stood there. I even snuck into the bathroom once and watched him brush his teeth. He used a greenish powder instead of toothpaste, which turned his teeth black. He was vegetarian and never drank Coca Cola. 'Til then, I had never heard of people not eating meat. How did they manage?

On Monday, at school, my classmates flocked to my desk and showered me with questions about the American. They couldn't believe that he brushed his teeth with green powder and didn't eat meat. *That wasn't a real one,* they said, *everyone knows all they eat is steak!* I shrugged my shoulders. What did they know, I had met an American —and they never would!

-First published by *Pure Slush* (Australia), 8 January 2011.

NIKKI ALLEN

baby teeth

meteor hips &
thin pick
long neck and short stack,
alternating sips
between life story summaries
—the good parts, by which i mean
the ones that sting,
dogeared and underlined
where we don't look particularly good
but
we look like ourselves.
i'll leave and after
send would'ves & should'ves
burned neon across my heart
billboard love blushing

i have the biggest dream
stuck in my teeth
do your worst
i won't smile.

open plan

maybe i need to stop calling my heart a house full of rooms, maybe its never been a segmented shelter. maybe there were never doors, only windows. what does a person call that? maybe the entire thing is underwater or almost, or maybe its drifting luxurious among space junk and rocket bits. maybe there isn't a roof or a floor and it isn't in space but *is* the abyss itself with frames of glass connected to nothing, and stars get stuck passing through and the dusty sheets drift off all forgotten furniture. maybe it is the busted chair end over end past jupiter, neptune, going going gone. maybe the dusty sheets wink into ash when they hit sun. maybe it's the amber drifting down to bite your arm. maybe it's the scar this leaves and maybe someone will trace slight keloid and want the back story. maybe it's too fantastic. or maybe you'll tell it, absurd tale measured out in beats per minute.

ode to ferric oxide

there were so many sad songs i forgot about. the ones reserved for road trips and roof sits. old gang hang outs you could reference when you caught it, random or not, on the sound waves. stories, real ones. they are fused round our condyles and we'll never shake them off. we are walking soundtracks and b-side believers

thicket of mixtapes. sectioning off entire evenings to get it right. meticulous block printed song list, plastic's sweat in my palm til handed off. but i was never a down-to-the-last-second-of-silence type of girl. unafraid of a sprawling live track wedged awkward in the middle. i'd leave a full minute of fuzzed quiet. i had the balls to cut a love song in half.

SANDRA FEEN

Youngest Bird

for Jenny, cancer survivor

She was looking for healing
decides concrete basement steps
map the right path to any answer
in an angel book.

A cry disrupts her gaze, the wanting
voice calls from an adjoining space
gutted also from Lancaster country earth

where the flue of a wood burning stove
traps a baby starling, forces him down to
the violating well of timber,
neglected logs.

Fingers pry feathers trembling
from the stove's black belly

and she reroutes her course
her hands a globe of fear
to the screeching creature of need,
once served as salvation's book opened
to the street corner cat with a back wound,
removed hooks from Fall Mountain Lake's fish,
then dipped them back into wet Connecticut.
Her hands aged from endless letting

animals go or endless leading
them to new habitats,

yet palms remember two other birds
unsaved from heavy pain, their nests of soil
between the tomatoes
and the sunflower patch.

Upstairs this beak pierces the early hour
and as his marrow feels the air of home
he waits, strangely silent and still
as the forgotten book.
She guides him past the golden bark
of the last mongrel who found her
and her fingers loosen, slow
as morning glory petals in their yawn.
And while his wings regain confidence
to the ascent,
her bones know well that sometimes
the youngest bird learns
the hardest lesson
and lives.

Flight
for Mal

Some people stake permanence beneath our skin.
You dive in, stay decades,
taunt private sea-level of sleep.
I tried to itch you out of my system;
arm scars reveal years mocking futile attempts.

Today, only three aisle seats separate us
on a Delta flight to Atlanta.
I know the back of your head,
lean left to watch you replay
the weird twist of your left ankle,
guess correct what you'd wear:
discern thin band of yellow gold, so
opposite the thickness of white
on my left-hand writing

this unexpected texture of flight
that prayer has come to
this: contained in sky thousands of feet
an attendant passes my note card
that asks, reclaims connection,
in a compartment of 50 strangers
that will hear us say what wasn't said
a precise 19 years before, in a misguided room
of two on solid ground.

This isn't about grand coincidence;
(forgiveness threads itself patterns
infinitely complex) or about words
fluttering into sudden air, after
loud casket of years. Reader, this
moment births epiphany, a moral on this page:
yesterday's tragic suppression may spin
you down corridors coarse, perhaps false;
there is no time to blink. Be ruled
by urgency of now; dare voice
what vibe imbeds down deep.
Sometimes you have to yank the drawer
so far until it spills on your lap,
no matter what you've been taught, or else

endure the tired fabric of regret;
live interrupted sleep, guilted dreams.

Your sky may not eclipse hinges, may not grant release.

Middle Age Fit

If you could sidle into that building naked, you'd do it.
Somehow, even a slim joke of sleeveless linen or cotton
weights you three pounds heavier; the car ride
from the driveway to Jenny Craig
wills your butt more time to spread
another fourth pound into day; don't dare
allow lips to touch that water bottle caressed
in the console beside you; wearing jewelry
is out of the question.

You enter a lobby of eggbeater yellow walls.
Kirstie Alley pinups stretch every inch
of her waning cleavage, of her Academy Award
red carpet dress, her mantra,
Yummy Jenny Craig brownies
for my new flat tummy
targets you, the poet, who can't stomach
forced rhyme or cheerfulness.

The diet police ushers you to step
onto your purgatory of numbers.
You haven't lost, so she has won
you, your dollars, for another week.
You proceed to her confessional, a room
thin enough for two, and you heave
this week's sugar sins; she documents
every addicted chip movement,
every buttered excuse, her breath, uneven,
she breaks pencil lead on a record your thirsting
eyes will never be privy to sip.

You choose food from a list that skips flavor;
petite portions in institutional caramel brown
are placed into your white bag.
You are directed to write everything down—
cough up your diary of morsels at week's end.
May I see less of you next week,
she spats sweet as syrup, and you drive
to a home where Richard Simmons waits,
his smile, cinnamon,
his brown sugar afro comfortable and constant
as his jellybean blue muscle shirt and shorts.
You find his entourage jumping behind him
refreshing, since they are vaster than the sizes
stocked in your bedroom closet, though when you
sweat to the oldies with them, their mocha bangs
and licorice ponytails don't dampen,
instead stay a curious peanut brittle dry.
Yet they troupe smiling through their tonnage,
and their smiles look sincere under a spotlight
where they gulp sassy fame, quick and portly.

You puff through every fifties song long enough
to know the exact moment Richard misses a knee strut
in *Big Girls Don't Cry,* replaces it with his drizzle
of shimmies, long enough to notice one gal's hoop earring,
substantial as a pancake, fly off before Richard pants
Have we reached our target heart rate?, long enough
to swallow all their good and plenty idiosyncrasies,
as you toil harder and harder at squeezing a smaller fit
into middle age.

ROBIN FREELAND

Closure

I am the one who has fought
through my anger
to the still waters
of the other side
of the moon's gravitational pull

I am on the other side of the moon
and it is all light

Methusaline's Long Lost Loves

how lovely
progesterone, estrogen, and testosterone

I wish I'd rubbed you on my thighs
a fortnight and five centuries ago
when I was peri
men
a pausing
posterior to the unctious blood-letting
of my female mould

its egregiousness
no longer a part of my ministration.

it is strange indeed
to be likened unto a highlander
though not immortal yet
whose stations in life are stretched out
so a period yea
be forty years and three

(and by period
wee scummer
I do mean
the cursed thing)

a pregnancy might stretch out
neighboring
365 years
A year's day's worth of years
blessed children did precede me
into that more fertile field

I, the precursor
witnessed
both death and rebirth

Presently
I shed blood flower no more

the end of the endometrium lays nigh
curling tendrils of
fallopian tubules
over ripen ovarian seeds
convening into odious maximus

my kingdom for a drink from the fountain of youth
says the queen who sings
who wants to live forever

female fragile fundus amondo us
my ometrium is dead
on a rival

but the cream
aye!
this medicinal magic potion
of apothecarian creation

makes me mellow mood
and entergizes the pistons
promoting style
abandoning stigma

I feel like a planted pistil,
a kin to the hair of the dog
wood
con-sense you-all

Released

the greatest gifts
come from those we thought
loved us
when we are freed by knowing
they only loved their idea
and finally
we are freed
from the pleasing

WENDY RAINEY

Girlie Show

It's the spotlight glaring in my eyes
that saves me the sight of anyone's face.
While striding the stage I tear off my dress
and it flies up behind me like a pair of wings.
I imagine I'm strutting the roof of a high-rise
and when I look down
I see the rats and roaches crawling the surface of the earth,
I look up and I am blinded by the sun.

But I must tread the edge of the skyscraper in stiletto heels,
naked,
my wings spread behind me,
the music blaring,
lifting me above the laughter of the hyenas
as they feed, and drink,
and watch.

-first published in *Chiron Review*

Distraction

We've had to lie to my Mother,
my sister and I,
in order to transition her into assisted living.
She has a touch of dementia
and can't be left alone.
The years of 24/7 home care
have diminished her funds substantially.
The story we told her
is that a water pipe broke in the wall,
flooding her house.
The damage will take months to clean up and repair.
I just want to go home.
I'm sick of hearing that guy moan all night.
She nodded in the direction of her neighbor.
I don't belong here with all these creepy old farts.
I know, I tell her, putting my hand on hers.
If I don't get to go home soon,
I'll die.
I know I will.

Trying to distract her,
I pulled out some photographs from an old Buffums box.
There were several of my stepfather, Steve, when he was young.
Steve used to screw the waitresses
who worked at that coffee shop he always hung out at.
I looked at her,
my mouth falling open.

Dad screwed waitresses?
She laughed.
You're not upset?
Well, not anymore. That was years ago.
Besides, I have no right to be.
She picked up a Polaroid,
studying it with a magnifying glass.
She was dancing with her gardener,
Hector,
his arm around her waist,
her skirt twirling up.
Steve's head didn't make it into the photo,
but I could see his hands lifting
a bare midriff.
A pair of tanned legs in red stilettos
flew in the air.

She threw the photo onto her bed.
I watched her grab the bottle of Merlot
on her nightstand,
pouring it into a crystal goblet
that I had brought from her house.
A voice called *Bingo* from the nearby rec room.
Her hand shook as she lifted the glass,
downing the wine in a couple of gulps.
I'm not one of them, she said,
pointing at an old man in a wheelchair
rolling by her open door.
Goddammit, can't you see I'm not one of them?

-first published in *Missing Persons: reflections on dementia.*

Comfort Pet

I see her out for a stroll with her Chow Chow
at South Coast Plaza,
strutting through Nordstrom
in pink stilettos,
white leather pants,
breasts barely contained in bodice,
Hermes scarf
tied to Birkin bag,
long black braids
swaying to the rhythm of her buttocks.
Her eyes fixed on a distant planet.
Her heels walking across the backs of men
to a life of ease and comfort.

I look at my own reflection
in the glass doors at Bloomingdale's
and imagine myself
rising from the mist of a bog,
smearing mud across my naked body,
blue paint in my hair,
holding a spear in one hand,
and an iron chain in the other,
at the end of which
is a starving lion.
I unleash him in lingerie,
take a seat
and watch.

TRINA DROTAR

Hart Island

Four days each week a lone,
unmarked, refrigeration truck
delivers, by way of ferry, the
goods to New York's second
largest city.

Unsalable product exchanged
for paper where hours aren't
posted, where signs for the
800,000 plus cartons list no
name, expiration date, or
contents.

The island's rhythm rises during
epidemic, during hard times. No
dancing or swaying as stillborns
meet the poor who lie next to those
cut off from family, from friends.

Words of prayer one Thursday
every   other   month.

Cutting

1.

A thirteen-year-old girl stumbles
down stairs in sleep shirt and shorts,
knocks over a picture of someone's relative.

Her foot bleeds while her brother imagines
clowns dancing and laughing and blowing balloons
that look like swords and dragons and poodles.

She bandages her foot with a cloth
found on the floor by her sister's boyfriend
while her mother yells
the girl places her hands over her ears and
accepts
a glass shard from the boyfriend.

2.

She turns seventeen, arms and legs bear
abstract designs – maps and tales.
Right upper thigh and left forearm
trace her junior year at the third high
school. Left bicep tells of nine months
when she turned fourteen.

The boyfriend's name linked
to the dead child.
Both calves reveal truths
about the scars that bloomed
on her back, the monthly black eyes,
the Sunday nights spent with her father.

The brother no longer dreams of clowns.

3.

Now a woman of thirty-two, she stands
before a grave. Her mother's name carved
into granite.

Dead eight years.

Her father never tends the grave. He still drinks,
and the brother dreams of swords and dragons and
poodles sliced and burned and he dreams
that he is the dragon, that he can fly, that he holds
the sword.

4.

She lives in a room in a house with
a man. They had not married.
He had found her collapsed
and he had taken her home and tended her wounds

and he had washed her hair and cut it
and he had washed her fingers and toes,
    gliding the washcloth between each digit,
and he had placed her in a bed that was not his
and he had pulled the cover up
and he had lit a lamp.

The Blue Shirt
for Keith

The man said to walk away,
even if it was his relative. Did
you ever know me to back down?
Of course I had to look, had to know
you had been living, surviving.

When did you begin reading
C.S. Lewis, the Bible, and about
heavy metal bands?

Crates stacked formed bookcases
behind a television on the hardwood
floor – why hardwood in an apartment
on the wrong side of the wrong side
of the tracks that employed people
can't even afford. A leather sofa opposite
the bed, but there was supposed to be a chair.
No room for a chair. No closet. The fridge empty
save for two hotline magnets. He said
that you'd made more than a century's
attempt by overdose,
with sharp objects,
and at least once by jumping
off a multi-story building.
A wet backpack nearly missed contained
notepads,
        tobacco,
and socks.

Where was your toothbrush, toothpaste?

Who gave you the stuffed teddy bear with
HUGS on the front and *2010* on one arm,
the black stuffed horse? The only new items
in the room, they'd been placed on the sofa
back, and in the bathroom, a ring on a jar
on a table with a drawer of tools – your
treasures – and the blue shirt (it matched
your eyes) hanging from the vanity mirror.

JYL ANAIS

No Trespassing

One day, I'll walk
without invitations for rides
shouted by men in
pickup trucks
driving in the opposite direction.
Straight to Hell.

And wait for a bus
without an incessant flow of questions
regarding my marital status &
whether I've been incarcerated
or not, as though that
would explain why
I'm not married
yet,
if I'm looking for a boyfriend
and why not,
whether I'll take their phone numbers
to call when I'm ready
for one.
Constant harassment
imbeds itself
in me.

I think I'll tattoo
No Trespassing
across my chest
after all,
and walk with
a pit bull named *Happy*
my body between
sandwich boards that read,
like the sign
in Isabel's bedroom did,

No hunting
or fishing, here.

Empty / Rising Tide

It was a day
of waiting
and a spot
a touch of blood

shed,
a release
letting go of what was
no longer needed.

I waited for you
and there was nothing
but silence.

Today, my body is also
silent
my womb empty
with nothing more to let go of
and I wonder
what I said that evoked
this silent night.

Images of a water table
and the vast expanse of embryonic
fluid that makes the earth inhabitable
and the ocean floor is where I sit
and create, from

the womb that is emptying
into another stage of life's journey
and the release I want to feel with you
like the swell
of a rising tide.
My womb,
the holy grail.

re(member)

I remember
myself piece
by piece.
How
does a woman
forget
she wears perfume
to sleep?

LAUREN SCHARHAG

The Macaws

Mi abuelo brought a pair of scarlet macaws
back from Mexico one year. I imagine he thought
their rainbow-colored plumage would help carry him
through the bleak Midwest winters, a reminder of home.
He built a cage for them of scrap lumber
and chicken wire and put them in the sun.
He fed them a rich diet of fruits and nuts.
Yet, they squawked all night long,
even when their cage was covered with blankets.
They had been wild-caught,
and never stopped honking their outrage
for the loss of their tropical nativity, for lychee and guava,
for eggs that Abuela didn't carefully boil
and slip back into the nest of newspapers
beneath the female's tail feathers. Instead, they had fleas,
a corner of the living room with its wood-paneled walls,
a single maiden-hair fern in macramé,
and a view of the blue-collar street beyond.
The floor around their cage was covered
in walnut shells and rinds and shit.
In the summer, they were moved to the back porch,
and one day, fed up with avian infanticide and sleepless nights,
Abuela left their cage open. Now, I see news articles
about parrot colonies from Miami all the way to New York,
birds of paradise roosting in palm and oak alike,
thriving anywhere that gardeners offer up flower

and fruit trees, power lines succumbing
beneath the weight of their nests, whole electrical grids
wiped out by their persistence of being, while back in the tropics,
deforestation is killing their kind. And then I understand
why Abuelo related to these birds so well:
in a new country, he found a bed, a mate, the flower,
the fruit, and the meat of the nut. He found a way
to birth generations.

Epigenetics

An evacuee from a hurricane,
I reflect on the life of my great-great-grandmother,
fleeing Mexico. Only she was fleeing something
far worse. It was 1918.
The influenza had struck her little Michoacán town,
taking her husband and six of her seven children.
It took everyone except her mother, her sister,
her brother-in-law, and her one remaining son,
who would become my great-grandfather.
Like some strange proto-apocalypse film,
she gathered up her plucky little band of survivors
and struck out north. In those days, it seems,
the border was far more tenuous.
They paid a nickel a person, (or was it a dime?).
Some nominal fee to pass over the bridge to Laredo
and claim a new home.
I don't mean to imply that it was easy.
I have no idea how they made it over 1,000 miles
to the border. Then, once they were here, *al otro lado,*
they worked their way steadily northward,
working in kitchens, in laundries. They sold tortillas
by the roadside, they told fortunes.
It took them two years to make it to the Midwest.
I can't imagine losing so much, even now,
with category four winds bearing down.

But I have my family. I have my car,
my citizenship, my insurance,
my American Express. I wonder what my
rock-bottom looks like, if I have inherited
any of my forebears' talent for survival.
I hope I never have to find out.

Inheritance

Sometimes, I wonder
what I would've taught
my grandchildren.
My own grandmothers
were not like
everybody else's grandmothers.
They cussed and brawled and
got thrown in drunk tanks and
told dirty jokes and laughed
raucously and wore
lots of eye makeup.
I like to think
I would teach you
the grandmotherly things
that I've read about:
how to bake cookies,
how to collect buttons in a jar,
how to reuse margarine tubs
instead of Tupperware.
I don't know how to quilt
or knit or anything,
but I do know
how to love fiercely,
unapologetically,
and to be who I am.
I like to think
I would have
passed that along
as well.

MAUREEN SHERBONDY

The Bridge Crossing

A sign for the Delaware Memorial Bridge appears. June approaches the tollbooth. She had never driven the bridge alone. Ronald, her husband, had always said, *You can open your eyes now* when the car finally reached level ground, the expansive bridge behind them.

Her hands tremble as she stops and faces the young tollbooth attendant.

"How much is it?" June asks, trying to steady her hands long enough to pull money from her purse.

The attendant, a thirty-something blonde-haired woman, is about the age of her daughter Suzi, who gave birth to twins just last week. This is why June is traveling over this bridge. Her sleep-deprived daughter had pleaded for help over the phone.

"Mom, please, please, come out for a few days. Tommy's back at work and I haven't slept. Ronnie's up every hour and Reagan, she's up every two hours."

June stares at the butterfly and rainbow tattoos on the attendant's arm. This is where the similarities end. Suzi is clean-cut, the girl-next-door, clothed in Anne Taylor or Gap casual.

The attendant chews her gum. "Eight dollars," which sounds more like *dollahs*. June wrangles with her wallet and finds a five and three singles, then she stays put. Eight dollars seems like a lot of money for a toll. Ronnie always took care of those money things. At her home in Havre de Grace, a pile of unopened bills waits on her dresser. She hasn't even found the checkbook yet. Who could focus on something as trivial as bill paying with all that's been going on? At the funeral home, Suzi had wobbled around nine months pregnant taking care of the details and expenses.

"Thanks. You have a question?" The attendant glances at the line forming behind June's Buick Regal.

"Oh. Um. After the bridge do I get in the right or left lane?"

"Depends where you're going. Miss, I need you to move ahead. Don't you have a GPS system on your phone?"

"Yes, that's right. Okay. Thanks." June presses the pedal softly.

If Ronald were here, they'd have been at Suzi's side the day of the twins' birth. But it's taken five sleep-deprived days of therapy to prepare for this journey.

June turns on the relaxation CD. The sound of soft triangles echoes and a slow deep voice says, *Breathe in, hold it for five seconds, breathe out.* The ocean waves begin. She takes a breath, holds it, exhales. Empty pots and bags of soil rattle in the backseat. The scent of potting soil relaxes her. Yesterday, June planted rose bushes on the side of the house, red ones to honor her husband's favorite color. Friends called him Red because of his hair. Her nail beds are lined with leftover dirt. The thought of digging dirt from the ground relaxes June. A few months before when June was cutting back bushes, Ronald had come outside, removed the cigar from his mouth and said, "When you finish this, can you come inside so I can go through the bills with you? I'll show you where the will is and the important account numbers."

She'd taken the cigar from his hand. "This is bad for that heart of yours, honey. You don't need to show me that stuff now. Another day."

But another day had never come. His heart valve replacement that night.

The bridge looms in the distance. A sign for 295/NJ Turnpike in green stares at her. Cars zoom by and she grips the wheel tighter. She drives forward, squeezing her right hand, imagining the cool earth in her palm. The scent of soil in the backseat rises again. June pictures stems emerging from the soil and purple flowers opening.

There are four stanchions in the sky, wires draping down like webs. She feels like a spider seeking out a safe corner. At the last exit before the bridge, June sees four confusing arrows. Which lane should she be in? Too many choices. It reminds her of the sample coffins lined up with their different colors and wood types.

An emergency call number appears on a different overhead sign. How would she call that number while driving over the bridge?

The stanchions remind her of the Catholic church she and Ronald were married in. That was more than forty years ago. They had gone religiously when their daughter was young. After she went away to the University of Delaware, she and Ronald stopped going to services. She never believed in the power of prayer. If she made it over this bridge, she promised church would enter her life again.

"Damn you, Ronald!"

She moves slowly along in the far-right lane up the incline. Then she makes the mistake of looking to the right: water. What if she falls in? Who will save her?

There is no shoulder, only a thin metal line with open grates. At the top of the bridge she slows and then hits her brakes. Cars screech. She hears beeping all around her. June covers her ears and closes her eyes. *Breathe in, breathe out,* the voice says. She turns the CD off. Even the voice is too much. Sweat drips from her forehead. She cannot move. The beeping continues. She holds her shaking hands over her ears as hard as she can.

A loud knocking at the window startles her. A voice. "Ma'am. Ma'am. Are you okay?"

She opens her eyes. A young man in uniform stands on the open metal grid. He bangs on the passenger window.

June unlocks the door. He has kind brown eyes like Ronald.

"Ma'am, I'm Petty Officer Thomas. Are you sick?"

"The bridge. I can't." June keeps her hands on the wheel.

"Why are you up here?"

"Ronald drives. I don't drive. Suzi had twins and needs me."

"Where's Ronald?"

June shakes her head. "Last month. The valve didn't work. Ronald always drives over the bridge. I close my eyes. He tells me when it's over."

The beeping is so loud she has to yell so the officer can hear.

She looks behind her car and sees a military vehicle. Petty Officer Thomas waves to the man at the wheel.

"Stay put. I'll be back."

"Where would I go?"

He speaks to the driver, then returns to her passenger side.

"Could you drive me, Mr. Thomas?"

"You're going to drive us over this bridge. I am going to be right here talking you through it. First time's the hardest. May I sit here?" He points to the empty seat. June nods and Petty Officer Thomas climbs in.

"I can't."

"Yes, you can." Petty Officer Thomas holds her trembling hands. "My mother was also a gardener. And she was afraid of swimming and water. I took her out on my boat and made her drive. I held her hand just like this. She was never afraid of water again after that."

June looks at him. "Those twins need me. Suzi needs me."

"Eyes ahead. Let's go."

June thinks about all the other bridges that wait for her. How will she make the next journey without a man beside her to talk her through? How will she navigate bill paying, house maintenance, and loneliness? Can these same hands that tend to a thriving garden get her through the next twenty years alone? Petty Officer Thomas squeezes her hand.

Together they continue over the bridge until the road flattens. Her heart slows when she enters the green cradle of trees and fields. She pulls over. She hugs Petty Officer Thomas, then wipes the dirt from her nails and recalls Ronald's coffin lowering into the earth.

K.R. MORRISON

Lady Viking

A tall and lanky woman with rings on every finger
once told me that her lungs warehouse snare drums
closest to an artery that one way streets to her decisions.

Of course, we became fast friends.
And next to her, I imagined a world where we women
could be free to love one another purely
the kind of friendship that when holding hands
rings go forgotten, fingers grow confused.

This world is possible.
Ladies with gas lamps tucked inside ribcages
torches blazing inside our thighs
highways made by our bare feet
scarlet fire seasons chronicled
by sapphire and garnet around our heads.

I cannot tell my new friend this.
So instead, I wrote her a love letter on a bar napkin.

> *Dear Lady Viking,*
> *I want to climb into your mouth*
> *salvage your tired words that retire*
> *below a rooftop of memory*
> *made of you and me. With you*

I want to hold female gravity in my hand
swim inside your burning stomach
listen to your loud heart in a seashell
roosting in a lost man's ears.

Life Letter to Anne Sexton

If the living dead and the dying stuck here
could trade Kraft slices for autographs,
I'd meet you

>in my living room –
>where countless books
>soundtrack shelves of music
>memorized by my veins, diary landscape
>where a woman's gumption
>breathes, confronts The Patriarchy's blaze

Our skin burning, we'd be two lady heretics
trapped inside mice bodies, seeking
rabbit holes in hardwood floors
until we find yellow wallpaper
to graffitti, then burn it all black
while holding hands –
>holding words –
>>poem in poem.

The truth is, you and I visit all the time.

>I meet you between the lines
>of *Live or Die*, basketcases of poems
>where I'm frozen in the 3rd grade
>trapped in department store dresses
>and pearls, my stomach purging
>rainstorms, shrouded in mother triggers

If I knew how to stop what hurts you
        the hurricaned field of apricots
        the blackbird lynched to a thriving oak tree
        your relentless dance with Mr. Darkness
                while everyone else stays so happy
                inside life seasons, so sure of Man's Day
                        well then I wouldn't have you, would I?

I'd lose the war that makes words get a life,
Sexton resin urging one restless girl to rise.
I'd forfeit the fire inside me, the fury
of the SCUMGIRL Collective underpants.

To your surprise, irony is an afterlife.

        Without your poems,
        bloody wrists in bathtubs
        or carbon monoxide catnaps
        would be many a girl's memoir, as you know
        an unfortunate departure. I know
        for me, retiring to eternal moonlight
        would be a tempting wilderness

if you weren't here, breathing

        inside these books, whispering to girls
        enlivened by word retreats.
        Maybe between the lines
        of your free verse resides
        your beloved Mercy Street.

Witch Poet

Before he hijacked her diction
she wrote for topics that matter —

>   mother's starving
>   for more wombs, black
>   eyed bruise cruisers
>   and scathed street kids
>   wishes blocked from sunburns
>   worded by winter.

Now, under his spell
her word revolutions wait
while she prostitutes
for male pronouns.

But poets needn't worry —

>   whores either die or they recover
>   in the wake of a heretic's regret
>   they resurrect as a Serengeti elephant
>
>   guiding damaged girls back to dictionaries
>   for a little witchcraft, for a cauldron
>   stinking of rich diction, self-respect.

Strong blood from her pen returns her
to summon Amazons, haunting him
in sleep, in manuscripts.

Her words. Such spells
escort her back, her words
burn him in the fire
she conjured him

HEATHER SULLIVAN

Cavern

My heart rings hollow,
scooped out by a melon baller
with each impassioned strike,
flayed open by the pretty
seventeen year old with the
dark brown pony tail standing
at the gelato counter. Her wrists,
not so delicate, clean even the
farthest corners, the tiny silver
bell on her anklet jingling when
she leans in. This heart, smooth
and thin as Mongolian beef on
the plate, barely moves the
blood anymore, hardly twitches
in a century, manages to pulse
for a moment at your touch.

Where Wisdom Comes From

The water is
calling me home,
this tug of osmosis
pulling at my fingernails,
telling me how close
the ocean is and how
equilibrium is possible.
Less than a half mile away,
the walk would barely
warm my calves,
even at a brisk pace.
Survival on this rock
is predicated on gaining
the high ground,
Obi Wan tells us that.
At the water's edge,
wisdom comes from
knowing when to stop
walking forward.

Mama Loves You

I'm sitting on the blood-red
cherry blossom conference center carpet
trying to tease out another 5% charge
on my phone, so that my messages
to you will float through time and
space unimpeded.
The woman tethered to the wall
beside me chants,
   Mama loves you
   Mama loves you
   Mama loves you
like a mantra to the toddler on the
other end of her tin can rope.
She needs so desperately to hear
the returning answered prayer
to the bright flags swinging
in these Nepalese winds,
the hope that the high timbered voice
on the other side
will prove that she isn't forgotten,
that there is no out of sight out of mind.
To address the fear is to have it erased.

ELLARAINE LOCKIE

Sexed on a Kona Balcony

All his lovers have fed the birds he says
This is after I've sprinkled the balcony
with pieces of pancake

Well, we can't help it
Our wombs command the role
as surely as the moon dictates the slap
of waves against lava rock below the hotel

We are hardwired to feed hunger, if not in children
then in pets, plants and wild things
I especially like the wild ones
The touch between feral and female
A scrap becoming energy that burns in both directions

The myna who is empowered to squawk and walk
the perimeter as if giving orders
Zebra doves too dumb or smart to pay attention
House sparrows hopping like wind-up toys
as they pick up pieces for babies in a nearby palm

All of them fueling to follow their own destinies
And me with the same small flame that must have
kindled Annapurna when she filled Shiva's begging bowl
It burns through my morning bath

When I come out wrapped in a towel
A saffron finch with fluorescent head
is eating macadamia nuts
that my man chopped with his pocket knife
He calls it male bonding
The nuts are coffee-coated, sugared and salted

First published in Heavy Bear

Should Have Been a Boy

She should have been a left-handed cowboy
But her mother wouldn't hear of it
Although she let the girl cross-dress
without slapping the offending boots, hat
holsters and gun every time
they reached out for approval

Now it's dreams where she has a penis
and cowboy boots that keep the boy alive
He breathes even under the six feet of dirt
shoveled by conformity

She feels him stir as she slips feet into boots
Toes no longer pointed into stirrups
where slant of high heel secured them
Where they'd ride the range, corrals
and cow trails far from patted-down
town roads and city pavement

Here they look up into mini-skirt
sarong or business suit
They fly to foreign countries and attend
formal dinner dances
Yet still squeeze black jeans into a yearning
Not for the rhinestone studded
confetti colored cowboy boot stampede
in Nashville, Melrose Place or Fifth Avenue

But for the Montana boy in her
The boy keeps her grounded in bloodlines
that seep through country soil
Pulls her back to where cowboy boots
hold up spurs and stop saddle chafing
Where they pound dirt into dust
mud into muck and snow into slush
Powerful enough to be declared
a lethal weapon in a Montana court of law
But the boy isn't concerned
He'll always be underage

First published in Main Street Rag

Taking Issue with Marcelino

who suggests a boy flex his forearm
instead of shoulder when he fingers a girl
A forearm, like he's pulling a calf
Let there be light in the darkened corner of the barn

Where a girl waits for the haystack-lush
breeze-through-chokecherry bush touch
from her first boyfriend
A boy who perhaps works at the post office
where he spits on a finger
and pets a stamp onto an under-paid envelope

Or maybe his mother introduced him
as a child to the art of fingerpainting
When he learned to ease fire engine red
into the pink of an earthworm's crawl
Into flush of cheek and slush of melting snow
with the cursive of one slow O after another

Or let's say he plays Chopin late at night
after his garage band practice
Taps the keys with feather tips
How he holds the hammer inside
Turns the slams against his heart into a prayer

Like a priest saves himself for Christ
Knowing the sacrifice will be rewarded in the end

The way lightning explodes over the night prairie
Blesses both the boy and girl through the one window
and blinds even the stars with their brilliance

First published in Ibbetson Street

AGNES VOJTA

Peace of the River

I want to spend a year by the river
and live in her seasons, wake and sleep
each day to her music, sense her mood
from the sounds and smells.

I would be up early to see the mists
rise from the water and to watch
the great heron wade in the shallows.

I would walk on the banks at dusk
and wait for the bats
to emerge from the cliffs.

I would listen to the muddy torrent
after the winter rains
that warns me to keep my distance,

and to her languid green summer voice
that beckons me to throw myself into her arms,
trusting her to carry me past the jungled bluffs.

I would let myself be cleansed and blessed,
and the peace of the river would fill my soul.
I could never leave again.

We, the Argonauts

We crawled from our boats,
tired from drifting through chaos,
to rest on an island in space and time:
tonight, we are safe.

We are a haphazard band of travelers,
each carrying our own scars,
our personal brand of crazy,
our deep humanity,
and our flawed loves.

For a while, we are companions
in a fellowship of seekers,
look for answers at the bottom
of the river or the bottle
or in the inscrutable face
of the oblivious moon.

Perhaps the golden fleece
is just a phantom,
and we are meant to remain here,
where the river flows in steady blessing
and night is a symphony of frog song.

Alea Iacta Est

I lingered
on the banks of the Rubicon
as if it were the River Styx
and I afraid of the final ferry ride,

but the die was cast
the moment I admitted to myself
what I had carried deep inside,
and started speaking it,
softly and with hesitation,

and I crossed the Rubicon,
and instead of dim Asphodel Meadows,
green fields with unforged paths
lay waiting.

BARBARA MARIE MINNEY

Real Woman

I may never be accepted
   as a real woman
I have not walked
   a mile in their high heels
   …nor do I claim to
I am not trying to misappropriate
   their womanhood
   …but I am laying claim to my own
I will never know
   the delights of being a little girl
   or the struggles of being a woman
   but my own struggles are real
   …and they matter
Womanhood chose me
   I did not choose it
   it was always inside me
   it was always me
   …even when I did not claim it
I am a trans woman
   and may always have that qualifier
   dysphoria is what sets me apart
I will always look in the mirror
   and see the remnants
   of the man I was.

The Ornament

Little girls in
   pink and blue dresses,
   lots of ribbons and bows
   and flowing tresses,
   innocence in their eyes
   and joy on their faces,
   dancing around the Christmas tree
   in delightful embraces.

I am drawn to
   the ornament hanging in the store,
   leaving my friends,
   and the present,
   to wander into their circle,
   dancing with them,
   as the little girl
   in a frilly dress
   that I never was.

Kintsugi

I treat my breakage
  as part of my history
  there is little use

in disguising it
   embracing my flaws
     and imperfections
highlighting my cracks
   and repairs
visualizing my mends and seams

joining myself back together
   with gold and silver of experience
like a kintsugi artist
   not allowing my service to end
     being reborn as a masterpiece.

D.C. BUSCHMANN

Gossip

A snake lurks
in the dark

infuses carriers
with venom

sinks fangs into
prey
       by proxy.

Nature's Irony

I shrink at
the child-like shrieks
the rabbit makes
scrambling
under the fence,
as the schnauzer
sinks fangs
into its all white meat—

the same fangs
inside a furry face
that habitually
snuggles
under my chin,
purring
like a kitten.

Nature's Medicine

after Langston Hughes' "April Rain Song"

Raindrops pelt glass and steel
in my parking space.
I wait, examine
bubbles and liquid shapes,

lean back, touch headrest,
close eyelids heavy as gravestones,
tell myself,
This deluge soon shall pass.

Nature, in her stride,
massages nerves
      splintered like wood
with her soothing lullaby

pitter patter

pitter patter,

pitter patter.

Elvis!

We were sisters, we were twins, we were Tom Sawyer and Huckleberry Finn. When Philomene and I were six years old we certainly weren't sissies. We weren't GIRLS!! All those books that Mother had given us to read... Mark Twain, Charles Dickens, James Fenimore Cooper, why were they always about boys? Boys must be better than girls. So we didn't want to be girls, we wanted to be boys. We couldn't actually *be* boys so we just said we were and played as if we were instead. So we became Tom Sawyer and Huckleberry Finn. We wore big straw hats, cut holes in our jeans, cut the hair off our dolls to make them boys, pretended that we were running away. When we were thirteen, Mother said we're going to get a new nice couch. It will be nice for when you start to have boyfriends come around we said *Eeeewwww, we are NEVER going to date BOYS!*

One year later we were dating boys. It was 1954 Bill Haley's "Rock Around the Clock" was released and Rock n' Roll was born. We were freshmen at The Academy of Our Lady of Peace. It was the most upscaled of the three Catholic girls schools in San Diego. The school was in Italian Renaissance style. Our uniforms were quite proper. We wore dark blue jackets and skirts, blue and white oxfords and a little badge saying OLP. $50,000 a year to go there now. Not then. But, we weren't all that proper. There was still a lot of Tom and Huck in us.

Rebellion was in the air. In 1956 Allen Ginsberg had read his poem HOWL which began the Beat generation. We spoke some poetry too. Like, *made in the shade* or *see you later alligator, after a while crocodile.* We loved Marlon Brando and James Dean. We were crushed when James Dean died. We too were rebels without a cause. The cool boys greased their hair back and had DAs or flattops. Of course those were the boys that we were interested in, went *steady* with, parked in cars and made out with.

We dressed in the 1950s usual sweater, bobby socks, flats. At the sock hops we wore longish skirts which would swing around when we did the jitterbug. Philomene had bleached bangs. I had my swinging ponytail. Rosie, who was our best friend, wore a DA that was bleached blonde and she was right up Philomene and my alley as far as getting into and making trouble.

Nothing serious. Minor things. Cut out of school for lunch. Have a PJ Party at Rosie's pad. Slip out the window and roam the streets in our PJs at night. We were *Cruisin' for a bruisin'*. We'd listened to rock 'n' roll 45s any chance we got. Philomene even invented a way we could keep repeating the same song automatically which drove Dad nuts. *I don't mind if they listen to music, but do they have to play the same song over and over again?*

April 3, 1956. Newspaper ad. *The San Diego Union.* In person Elvis Presley! Elvis sings "Heartbreak Hotel" "Blue Suede Shoes" other hits. Buy now. Save money. Advance tickets $1.25. At door $1.50.' It would be his first performance ever on the West Coast.

April 6, 1956. More than 5,000 screaming teenagers, mostly girls but some boys too, were jammed into The San Diego Arena. What a blast. He wasn't even on stage yet and things were crazy. We took our seats about fifteen rows back from the stage. I was on the aisle. Soon I was screaming too.

An announcer took the microphone and tried to get the 5000+ screamers to quieten down. Not much luck there. He warned that we could not get out of our seats and if we did the concert would end immediately. Elvis came out. The arena erupted. We, stomped, shuddered, shrieked and sighed as the young Elvis Presley *not to be televised below the waist pelvis Elvis* stood before us. He writhed his way through his first song. The whole place went hysterical. When the song ended he put his left arm up as if to calm us down and The San Diego Arena went dead silent. Elvis, softly, sweetly reminded us of what the announcer had said. *Y'all remember now you must stay in your seats.* Then he wiggled his little left finger in defiance and the entire arena burst out into a roar.

We quietened down again when he said in his sensuous secretive southern voice that he was now going to play a special new song for the first time just for us. It was called "Hound Dog." That was it. The place went wild. After the second line of the song I saw a couple of girls in the first few rows leave their seats. I thought if they were leaving their seats then soon everybody else was going to and I wanted to get there first. I got up and rushed down the near empty aisle. The entire stadium of 5000 got up and followed me.

There I was, right under him with the hysterical mob behind. He was up close and gorgeous and doing all that twisting and gyrating that the adults were so upset about. Then he suddenly stood still, pointed his right arm, looked me straight in the eye and sang *You ain't nothing but a hound dog crying all the time.* Time stopped. I was frozen. I could see and hear only him over the sounds of the screaming 5000. *You ain't never caught no rabbit and you ain't no friend of mine.* He finished the song and that was the end as the authorities did what they said they would do. They ushered Elvis off the stage and abruptly stopped the show. I stood there still shaking with excitement.

The San Diego Union reported… *Over both evenings, several young women were removed from the Arena, reportedly for "hysterical and lewd behavior."* Some girls broke into the bathroom of Elvis's dressing room and stole the toilet seat. After the concert, the police arrested 12 girls running nude through the halls of the El Cortez hotel looking for Elvis.

When Presley was scheduled to return to the arena June 6 the San Diego police chief blasted out, *If he puts on the same kind of show that he did last April, I'll arrest him for disorderly conduct* and, he was quoted saying in the San Diego Union repeated nationwide after newswires picked up the story, *I've had enough complaints from parents to show me that twerp is not doing the kids any good.*

That *twerp* Elvis was a rebel. Just like the Tom Sawyer and Huckleberry Finn we wanted to be. I didn't mind being a girl so much anymore. Not when there was an Elvis Presley around. At least for then. And he had told me I was nothing but a Hound Dog. That was certainly worth the $1.25 price of admission. Rebellion was in the air and I liked that. And there would be more to come.

LORETTA DIANE WALKER

Why I Am Jealous of Princess Diana of Themyscira, Aka Wonder Woman

She's a woman ravished by beauty—
78 years of age. No wrinkles. No fat. No pressure
for perfection, already more perfect
than a department store mannequin.
Puberty never scarred her face
with blotches, blemishes, blackheads.
I do not buy her T-shirt.
The power of her shield too flimsy
to heal the past of a bruised little girl
who wears a vacancy sign each day
where innocence used to live,
who she fights the myth
you're not enough because of your body
docked inside skin that blends with the night.

II
The right breast a full cup smaller than the left,
lashless eyelids and swollen arm are souvenirs
of chemo's crushing embrace.
Years sit heavy on my body.
Each day this receptacle of years
carries cancer relics.
Di's a cougar prowling
through this ceaseless jungle of time.
Emerges on the other side
with no scratches, scars, scabs of aging.

No ripples of cellulite on her butt or thighs.
Is this jealousy irrational?
I squeeze into a pair of tight jeans,
don black knee-high boots, walk
like the princess
my father never told me I am.

Waiting with a Stranger

He rivals Michelangelo's David
with his chiseled face, muscular physique,
boulder-hard biceps tattooed with a cross
and other symbols I can't decipher.
We stand outside a door where laughter bangs
hard against the wood. Our bodies too far for touch,
near enough to hear heavy inhales, exhales.

A Coach bag hangs from my shoulder,
a pink Hello Kitty from his.
His palms paddle in his pants pockets
as he shifts his weight with impatience.
We exchange glances in a sudden halo of silence.

A burst of noise. The door flings open,
a high-pitched voice screams *Daaadd-dy!*
I stare when he swoops up his cherub-nosed daughter.
Her response, a confirmation of ritual.
Thin arms clutch his thick neck.
Wheat-colored curls drape his left ear.
Small fingers fidget in the gully
of his wide back.
He christens her forehead with a quick peck.

A memory presses against my heart.
I am ten. June's blooming with heat.
My daddy, his new wife cruise beside me
with the smell of new leather wafting
through a partially lowered window.
With a faux smile she asks,
So, what did you get Robert for Father's Day?
With Body slouched, head dropped
like a drooping zinnia, I tell her, *Nothing*
as I reach for the back-door handle.
They drive away, wave,
leave me standing on the sidewalk
soaked in a well of shame.

Streams of laughing voices drench my memories.
Like a wet puppy, I shake the past until my mind
returns to the cheerful hallway where I waited
with a stranger I now dub Father of the Year.

When he walks away with his daughter, the little girl
inside of me cries, *Don't Leave. Please don't leave me!*

Why I Can't Keep a Lover

After I tell you innocence is not ripped out,
rather rammed into the psyche,

your eyes are like last night's hard rain.
Sometimes the story is the breaking

up.
I woke this morning

with my fingernails digging into my arm.
I dreamt you were falling

into the deep cavern of dark clouds.
You reached for me.

I was not trying to pull you out.
I was trying to thrust you deeper

into the darkness,
further away from the truth

of my broken skin.

STEPHANIE BRYANT ANDERSON

Cliff Tracks | Train Babies [I Always Wanted to Write a Poem About A Train]

but this isn't that. It's the oh-shit-I-can't-take-that-back.
It's the open pit in my stomach. The pig turning over its fire.
In the hole I fill images of young
me; I watch as I pick myself up. Set myself on my lap. My black hair, long.
My mouth not yet formed. Then or now. I am daughter /
    mother.
Babies, whose mothers don't care for them, don't watch them
    dream
of jumping the train   about freedom. They leap, the baby birds,
with their mouths open   but they don't make the train.
They cliff into soil and go away. Their flowerheads cut.
Now-Stephanie holds young-Stephanie.
Her mouth in braids. Mother taught her to keep secrets.
    To dive
into cliffs and soil. But, in my version young-Stephanie rises
a cornstalk / a beanstalk. She doesn't fall. Those mothers
broken. Or lazy with neighbors also broken. A neighborhood
where police also teach how the poor aren't worth the report –
from the time an adult punched my son, 9, in the stomach.
    They wanted
him to lift his shirt for the red marks. For proof a grown man
    hit him.
This isn't the story of David and Goliath: my son, the bigger
    boy, assumed
aggressor stood up to his bully.

His mouth has formed, though. Scared, his shivering voice says
ask the train about its howl. The howl is an answer back.
    A mother in hiccups.
A song of redemption and remorse. Those babies who leapt.
Those babies I couldn't save. The father of my baby who I
    couldn't save.
Young-Stephanie the first time around couldn't be saved
    from the hand
crawling into her five-year-old-shorts; from a man who took
    her hostage in
a yellow Volkswagen beetle and tried to rape her; from a man
    whose
fists like furious birds aimed for places on her body that others
    wouldn't see.
We are stuck in a dream loop where I keep searching for the
    right words
to tell them all how I felt. The right words to save everyone.
The sun dips its toes into night waters, and I am still in the loop
    trying
to say the right thing. All of my traumas looking for cliffs.

Of Radishes or Wounds

The hulled-out birds. The sleeping volcanoes.
When I told him   today you died
he said your dying   wasn't his problem.   At six years old
the sap's   irregular borders
shape like wild deer   and pink as hunting season.
Vegetables curating ground   my young corn-husk baby
chops at sugared water to make you sweet.
He tried to pull death from its mother   while other kids laughed.
The forest   the womb he stirred and made
from blood   asked for your body.   To nail down.
You were   already fire   and our boy
carrying   dead weight for far too long   didn't cry.
That summer   he spent in woods   carving
you from a tree and   next   pressed you into paper luminary
in hopes to see your face shine with copper   and love
but not flame   then he smothered   a field of fireflies to ash.

Here I Stand Horse Cropping Past
To Jenn Givhan

Where pain rots your belly, my forearms manipulate muscles
    to make a fist.
Or where I feel loneliness in open fields and dank woods
    where feared
witches conjured half creatures into my retinas. A tiny lung
    flower
grows emptiness lit by lightning bugs and thunderstorms
sometimes so intense to bring my spirit double. Breath like
    body manipulation, my
fault-line memory my mother says was never true: My ghost
    floats from mirrors
to the windows and into the cornfield where I whisper to
    anyone near enough
to listen: *I want to die.*   My boys catch a chipmunk,
    pull her
from the tree holding a home in its arms in its bouquet where
    my sisters
and I dressed up as mice wearing capes;   I secreted parts
    of my childhood
and soared across trees and chased bodies held in sun rays
in UFO abductions. Or church and rain.   I fell for the
    witchcraft, stories of The Bell witch and my father
stepped on the dreams where she called to me like a cockroach.
My bedroom holds no space, like bugs placed in a jar,
    moths, spiders, or snakes:
dead legs marking the sky in omen. I am rot: not worth

a womb or safety or touch.
I am her cave: your belly-cave and her bird-nest mouth.
   We mourn
the chipmunk who died from capture then set a trap for
   something bigger.
I was split from birth: from the body of a horse— where
   I am the whore.
On the other side of me stands a mirrored field of calves and
   utters.

NANCY P. DAVENPORT

Name-Calling Lasts Forever

did you know

that even during
my drinking   days

when   I   actually deserved   it

my   lovers didn't call   me   a   *bitch*

even my rapist
managed   to   call   me

by   my   first name

I was called *dog*

all through my childhood   do you think it can hurt me now?

but you have put it onto paper
made me   a   bitch

tried to immortalize me this   way

asked   me   to   edit   this

hey   fuck you   by the way
basically   crumpled up

a piece of

fucking paper   and   tossed it   into   my   face

okay   fine

but   you   need   to   remember

these things   they   stick
last forever

one reason why I've   relied on   names like
dumbshit   and   *dickwad*

you see now
in the   dark   of   night
bitch   is   what   I   hear

as you sleep
when you breathe in and out

not *sweetness*
not l*ove*
not *Nanny*

just   bitch

dickwad

Eclipse Indifference

the day of the eclipse
we go the   town fair

dance until   we tire
laugh until   our sides   stitch
discard shoes
and belt
to be   lost   forever

eat with sticky fingers

you leave barbecue sauce around
the buttonholes of
my white cotton blouse

town fiddlers   fiddle   crowd dances
a heedless immunity to the present

when night falls   finally
I go through the forest
behind my house

and as the silence gains in density
and the shadow falls
upon the moon

I dance   naked
with the
skunks   under the eclipse

scare the trees a little   bit

moon-mad

I am the only light out here

Sonora Pocket Poem #1

Flotsam, jetsam. It's hard to hear the music when you're stuck in the same groove. Hummingbird heart, monkey mind. If I could clap my hands together and make this all change, I would. But the same voices that called me at five and fifteen still call at two-weeks shy of fifty-five. A moment of clarity: it takes a finite amount of time to figure out the infinite. Water drips on this rock for years and changes the shape - but it's still a rock.

DIANNE BORSENIK

Fahrenheit
—*January 30, 2019*
—*after Josh Brooks*

Yesterday, he said his
nipples could cut glass,
and that's how cold it is

this morning. Wind chills
are currently minus
twenty-six, and dropping

steadily throughout the day.
All the news channels are
talking about an "arctic

blast" moving in a swath
across the States, with
the winds in our region

gusting at thirty miles
per hour. Tomorrow
should be a little better,

and the seven-day outlook
is insane, with temps
climbing into the fifties

on Tuesday. But today,
it's nipples-cutting-glass
frosty, and I'm braless.

It looks like I'm going to
need some new shirts,
come this weekend.

All That Jazz

Aging population resolves to keep its jazz,
becomes a congress of gray matter plus Gray Panther: sly
camouflage of colorful scarves and comfortable spandex,
delegates tuned in, turned on, outrageous and outlaw,
edges honed by experience sharper than a shiv,
fueled variously by weed, beef, tequila, and tofu.

Generational shockwave, this Baby Boomer cohort:
hippies, Spinners, classic rockers, thrashers,
iconoclasts questioning authority and parameter,
jaded marchers protesting political tranq,
keepers of faith, experimenters, change and shakeup,
lovers ever-seeking a bigger O,
monument to yesterday. Tomorrow's hymn.

When the Son of a Motherless Goat Tries to Stare You Down,

don't blink.
Don't even think of giving him the satisfaction
of a cowed reaction; don't little-down
yourself for a clown who's living in the past
century. Dismiss his attempts at intimidation,
ignore his dictatorial oration.
He's out-classed and can be out-sassed.

When the son of a motherless goat
tries to silence you, go full-throat,
full-throttle, head high and balls out,
bubble-pop his ego, Jericho his walls.
Let him stomp, let him stew, let him pout.
He may think he's God's greatest creation,
but he can't touch you.

When the son of a motherless goat
tries to get your goat,
don't let him. He isn't worth the hassle, not
for one minute. Stun him with indifference,
let him wonder at your grit.
Grin at his impotence. Don't grovel, float.
You've got this. Win.

BARONESS VON SMITH

Club Wasteland

The first time I heard Club Graceland called Club *Wasteland*, it came slurring out of my very own mouth as I sat around a beer-sticky table of divorced single-moms just like myself. None of us realized how old 38 was until we hit it. *I feel irrelevant,* Trisha would say, then finish her gin and tonic. Sandy would nod. *I don't know what matters anymore.*

Loneliness and co-misery drove us each down there in separate vehicles every Thursday night to drink, listen to the amateur DJ, and most of all watch Leon.

A glance at Leon led one to surmise there'd been some inbreeding, that his eventual wedding cake would be made from Twinkies, that he owned a deer's ass doorbell. But Leon possessed the kindness of angels and the hips of a slumming Adonis.

He moved along the tiny dance floor with heartbreaking grace, his western button-down shirts and golfer-plaid pants belying his toned, tan, mid-twenties body. *Dance with me, Mama* he'd coax, grinning gap-toothed. *Are you too good to dance with me?*

One at a time, he'd request our hands and we'd offer them up, Yes. He'd slip his college-age arm around our late-thirties waists and for a few minutes, the duration of a song, we'd feel like the queens we had all once been. Against the four-four time of three chord progression, Leon taught us the Cuban Rhumba's basic box steps, bestowed on us the Italian Tarantella's inherent mercurial adoration, even spoiled us with the twists and dips requisite of the Argentine Tango.

Leon hummed while he danced and when he didn't dance he talked. *I'm going away,* he promised. *I'm going out West.* He never said just what for. His friends thought him ugly. No one believed him. Nobody ever left, and if they did they came right back before year's end, full of excuses and fingers pointed in all directions except center. We nodded and smiled.

One Thursday, the DJ arrived and played record after record, and no Leon. He'd gone West we surmised, stunned. Done just what he said he was going to. Once he'd been gone a while we began to wonder if we'd invented him, participated in some group hallucination to stave the static sadness.

Leon hasn't come back yet and I don't believe he will, though no one has spotted him on a soap opera, or sit-com, or *Dancing with the Stars*. But it's been more than a year. No one dances at Club Wasteland anymore.

this small rain

this small rain sambas on San Vicente
wanders through Whittier
mambos past Montebello
and East LA

this small rain moves like a Latina
over-plucks her eyebrows
drinks Tequila shooters
fronts a girl-band

this small rain works two jobs
dawdles in down pours
this small rain seeds clouds

this small rain drives to Vegas in a tormenta
has a friend in Jesus
needs boots and a winter coat

in this drought-wracked city,
this small rain dreams of flash floods,
depósitos, indigo lakes,
cisterns, high water,
Big Gulps, endless refills

in this drought-wracked city,
this small rain settles on the yerba seca
sleeps under freeways
plays the lotto
is unlucky in love

this small rain longs to hose down the highways
this small rain chases storms

this small rain has a tsunami in her heart

this small rain kamikaze's
in the gutter
suicides on summer sidewalks
dreams of a deluge
that overflows the river banks
washes L.A. clean

in this drought-wracked city,
this small rain scans the heavens,
looking for a monsoon,
searching for su salvador in the
reclaimed desert sky.

yerba seca: dry grass
tormenta: rainstorm
su salvador: her savior
deposito: reservoir

Published in Get Lit, 2018

June Fairchild isn't dead

she's planning a comeback.
she's snorting Ajax for the camera.
she's landing a role on *I Spy*.
she's writing her number on a napkin and
handing it to me at King Eddy's Saloon.

June Fairchild isn't dead
she's just been voted Mardi Gras Girl at Aviation High.
she's acting in a movie with Roger Vadim.
she's gyrating at Gazarri's, doing the Watusi with Sam The Sham.
she's mainlining heroin in a cardboard box.

June Fairchild isn't dead
I saw her tying one on at King Eddy's Saloon.
she's making *Drive,* He Said," with Jack Nicholson.
she's selling the Daily News in front of the courthouse.
she's snorting Ajax for the camera.

June Fairchild isn't dead
she's relapsing in front of the Alexandria Hotel.
she's working as a taxi dancer, making $200 a shift.
I saw her vamping with Hefner, frugging on YouTube.
she's naming Danny Hutton's band 3 Dog Night.

June Fairchild isn't dead
she's living at the Roslyn SRO on Main.
she's giving up her daughter to her ex.
she's snorting Ajax for the camera.
she's planning a comeback, needs new headshots.

June Fairchild isn't dead
she's Up In Smoke, getting clean.
she's sitting by the phone.
she's falling asleep in Laurel Canyon
with a lit cigarette in her hand,
waiting for me to call.

Former Gazarri's dancer/film star June Fairchild, a self-proclaimed "angel in a snake pit," died of liver cancer on Feb. 17, 2015. She was 68 years old.

Published in Cleaver Magazine, 2016

Poem For The Girl Who Wanted To Stop Time

*when the sirens made apartment dogs keen,
she howled for him - her body a longing*

        *she gave away all her clothes
        she knew no one could love her
    *because he danced solo
    because she flew planes into mountains
    because she circled the drain*

*her Scorpio was in Venus; he'd left his in a stranger's bed.
        she needed what was left of him
        it was an inside job*

he wanted too much	*he didn't come home*
he couldn't choose	*he hated silence*
	he couldn't love

        *because she lived in the outfield
        because he feared the dark*
the trees were crying
        she stumbled and fell
*she couldn't take it
    back*
        *before she knew it, the stars had misaligned
        the moon was in Paris
        the astrologer smelled of beer*
*she'd lie if questioned
she knew the ropes*

she ate like a bird   *the shoes pinched*
the ocean waved   *he left her stranded*
the clock stopped   *she wanted to die*
he always left
she always forgave him

                                       now that he was dead
                                                 and
                                       that girl had disappeared.

First published in *Pirene's Fountain,* 2017

MICHELLE STORER

I found a letter you wrote
On the back of a storm
One of your suits was going to court
Phil got dumped
A postcard to his brother
From the Queen of Hearts
Caused fireworks bigger than Burghley House
Stolen images from
A ruined Abbey
Hidden amongst
A disorderly graveyard
When the lights went out
All you could do was feel
Through the wind and drizzle
And frightened birds

The wind blew
Silently through the
Bowed heads of
Dying roses
Expired tributes from the
Living to the dead
Trinkets and
Abandoned whiskey bottles
Stone chippings of
Emerald green
Miniature motorcycles and
Babies shoes
Amongst it all
The saddest thing
I ever saw
Footprints on
My mothers' grave
A thoroughfare for
Bastards
Who do not see
Or just don't care

She won't let him
Read my poems
She thinks they
Might contain
Secret messages
Unfinished business
Temptation or even
An escape route
From her paranoia
And control
She doesn't realise
That years of
Perfectly executed
Threats and fear
Have already created
Prison walls
From which
He will
Never escape
And borders
She no longer
Needs to patrol
Esteem suffocated
The job already done

Autobiography of a Pearl

> *All art is autobiographical. The pearl is the oyster's autobiography.* Federico Fellini

I became his pearl—
formed after the irritant
force fed into a shell,
not natural, not random.

A cultured pearl takes less time,
becomes uniform in size and shape,
desirable for ornamentation,
and so we strolled, me on his arm.

And everyone said how lucky I was
to be with a man so good-looking,
but handsome force fed me a diet
of grains of sand,

an oyster who wanted nothing
to upset his delicate constitution,
and so he covered me with nacre,
one layer after another

until I gleamed in a range of colors
resembling a peacock, but no,
that's the male with the spread
of fan of feathers.

I found a way to shine on a bay
known for what grows in estuaries,
what has always been there for larger fish,
some as big as whales.

But the whales had their day,
and still I was there inside the shell
until pried open by a knife at throat.
I had grown into a woman untouched

by hands of the harvester.
I came out at night, roamed the shore,
brought everything I had seen through gaps
in the shell, and scratched the story on walls.

I made note of everything—every woman
taken down to the sand and left until dawn,
every time he left town as soon as the round
of belly appeared, every child born.

And I followed those children,
nurtured them, fed them from the sea
and marsh until they grew enough fin
to swim away from here.

I did this for decades, a generation
in the lifetime of a pearl
cultured by a man as object
for all to see.

Woman With Pearls

We get on a bus—
my mother, me, my two daughters—
and go to Philadelphia, to the Museum of Art,
to see the first painting of a woman with pearls.

We climb the long stairs
not far from the Schuylkill River
and while it has kill in the Dutch name,
means hidden along banks of the Delaware.

We do this after we bury him in the front yard,
but not right away to arouse suspicion.
No one will be surprised to find him gone,
not even us and we know why.

We stuff all the pearls we can find
into his mouth. And there were a lot—
this bay known for beds of oyster
until a bacteria devastated the harvest.

The pearls made no sense at the time,
an act as irrational as the kill,
as irrational as what gets under your skin
that you keep trying to brush off,

but you can't reach it. It's buried too deep—
as he is.

Wilmington Stop

We spend a night in a modest hotel near 30th Street Station,
four of us in one room, catch a mid-morning train to Baltimore.

We go through Wilmington, stop to meet an old friend
who takes us to lunch, lends me some money, doesn't ask

questions. She never liked my husband, doesn't think
I should have married right out of high school, graduating

at top of my class. There is no way to tell her that a religious
background does not lend itself to love outside marriage,

much less sex. To even say it out loud seems judgmental
of her choices, and given our predicament more than a little

cockamamie, *so you're opposed to sex, but approve of murder.*
To make this all sound even more like something out of a play

by someone very French in Paris in the 1930s, she starts
telling us that she lives with two men, one her husband

and one her boyfriend. That the two of them were friends
before and have remained friends. That her husband sees

her lover as a father figure, the one he never really had.
I'm thinking, *so what do you see him as?* I do not ask.

FRANCINE WITTE

Breakthrough

You are bad at family dinners, those cattle calls
of memories and walking ghosts. You'd much rather
live in the now. What you want to call your grown-up

life. Instead, you are sitting across from Uncle Max,
dead in five years, who keeps shaking his head
at your mother, his younger sister, who, herself,
will be gone in two. How they thought you'd be married

by now, or famous. And you are nowhere near either.
You butter your bread, your go-to move. No eye contact
needed, and besides, the food is good.

Later, the train will rumble you home, back to your
one-room life with its stack of magazines and people
you are meaning to get to. But listen, one thing at a time.

First, there is a saying that today is the last day
of your childhood. And then, later, when you lie
down to sleep, be sure to close the curtain
on the moon staring at you through
the window like your mother's watching eye.

Any Other Street

would be made of asphalt, black pitch
pillowing in the August heat. But this street
is woven with bones and ash and anything else
leftover when a dream dies. It's the kind
of street you try to avoid when mapping
out directions. Once, for a party, I
entered a destination, and no matter
how many alternate routes I tried, this
street kept coming up. So all right,
I thought, I have a dream or two
I don't mind killing. I'll just dress
in them that day. But how was I to know
that life dreams are like night dreams,
and you don't get to choose? So, even
though I was willing to give up winning
the lottery or having my own reality show,
this street wouldn't be interested. It would
want that secret dream I had tucked away
down in my shoes. That dream of having
one simple day after another. It's not much
of a dream, but it's the one I really want.
A quiet sleep followed by not much of a morning.
Coffee going down to reliable cold. And I wanted
to keep that dream so much, I thought about turning
back. Who needs another party after all? But,

before I could turn around, that hidden dream,
maybe curious, maybe up for a challenge,
started to itch my feet, made me keep on
walking, maybe just to see how far
this street would really go.

Daylights

are being punched out
of someone, even now,

in a bar, perhaps, on the
edge of some steely, rust-

pocked town. Two old buddies,
beer-soaked and scrabbled.

Energy with no outlet, the daylights
sparkshower onto the floor, or

maybe it's the other kind, the daylights
that switch on the morning, that knifeblade

that blinds you and allows you to see.
Either way, the daylights are living,

and if you try to hide in your covers
or the arms of the wrong lover, the

daylights will shake you like an old
friend, who only called to have a beer

and can't believe it when you finally
confess to a moment of weakness,

his wife's pouty smile that time
he went out of town, how you

and she woke up to the loneliness stabbing
you both in the eyes. And rather than understanding,

the way you had hoped, there's a fist coming
straight at your face. Later, you are lying

flat out on the floor, your precious daylights
right there next to you, hissing and spitting

like some outsider to the sudden country
your body's become and is trying

to find its way back in.

TRINA STOLEC

Scarred for Life

Wood plank swings
sway empty in the wind.
Children are
lined along the fence...
riveted
to the strangest sight
they've ever seen...
an old man with a music box
and a monkey on a leash.
The monkey dances,
holds a cup to catch passing coins,
tips his hat
to the wind.
The old man
turns the music box crank,
smiles.
Wind rattles the swings
and the chain-link fence.

Mountain Graveyard

The slope is too steep for horse or mule,
the steps too narrow for planting.
So it became the graveyard…

For generations…
grass is moved,
weeds pulled,
headstones repaired.
Decorated on birthdays,
        anniversaries,
          dates of death.
On Memorial Day
the whole hillside riots with
        flowers,
        cards,
        toys,
        fond memories.
One family erects a wrought iron fence
around their baby's grave –
their way to preserve her resting place
forever and for all…

When the yard is full –
the families buried or
moved or
too old to walk the acclivity –
when a new place of rest
is found and tended,
the old one is forgotten…

Headstones worn by rain and wind,
toppled by roots of growing trees.
Graves sink in as coffins and contents rot,
    leave cavities in the earth.
A ten-foot tall tree grows in the middle
of the baby's wrought iron fence.
Weeds and
briars and
trees and
wild flowers
take over…
a jungle
with an occasional marker of the past,
because human life
is very good
fertilizer.

Nostalgia

I

We didn't have anything against
doorbells; we just didn't use them.
Stood at the neighbor's backdoor
and bellowed,
*OOOOOOOHHHHHHHH
DDDDDIIIAAAAANNNNEEEE*
until the requested bellowee
appeared at the screen door.
We'd lean close, conspiratorially ask,
Can you come out and play?

Grounded was real punishment.
You sit in your house-cell
hear the neighbors called out one by one;
hear them laugh, but not hear the joke;
hear them cry, but not hear who got left out;
hear them run, but not hear were to;
hear the ball bounce against the outside wall –
the distraction of muscle when a serious discussion
was afoot.
Or worse,
not hearing anything at all.

Now, hardwood stays shut.
The air conditioner's roar
drowns out the neighbor's barbecue.

My friends use the bell,
and the only time I hear,
*OOOOOOOOHHHHHHHHH
TTTTRRRRIIIIIIINNNNNAAAAA,*
it's my mind's whisper...
Can you come out and play?

II

There were three of us,
my sister Deb was the oldest,
Diane a year younger,
I was the baby they let tag along
so Mom wouldn't lecture my sister.
Being the youngest, I always got
last choice when we played.
Deb would be Batgirl,
Diane would be Batman,

I had to be Penguin –
deformed, caught in the act,
beaten up and hauled to jail.

It wasn't a storybook childhood, but
it wasn't as bad as being
one of the Smith kids.
The Smith's lived between us and Diane.
We'd run to the back fence
before crossing their yard,
scramble as fast as we could
so they wouldn't see us.

That's how I ran into the dog pen
the day they put it up.
It wasn't something I was expecting.
I mean,
my sister and I had to share a bedroom
and we considered that to be
cruel and unusual punishment,
but the Smith's had 12 kids
and only 3 bedrooms in the house.
And now they'd gotten a dog?

We were playing *Make Me Laugh*
on Diane's patio.
Deb was making faces;
I was trying hard not to laugh
'cause I always lost that game.
I tried to ignore
the contortions of my sister's face
without looking like I was ignoring her.
I saw Mrs. Smith come out
with three of the kids.
She walked to the dog pen,
opened the door.
The kids climbed inside.
Mrs. Smith locked the door
and went in the house.

The term *child abuse*
wasn't the catch phrase it is today,
and though the neighbors whispered,
I don't recall anyone saying that.

I remember thinking it wasn't right—
locking a kid up so they couldn't run.
I remember thinking grass shouldn't be seen
through the shadow of bars

when you're 8 years old.

Deb, Diane, and I
started spending time in their yard
singing Kumbaya and If I Had A Hammer.
holding fingers through the openings
in the silver metal squares.
We'd run when Mrs. Smith came out, though.
She'd unlock the pen door,
the kids would follow her inside
waving at us as they went.
We sat on the rusty swing set,
swayed back and forth
to creaking chains
until someone'd finally say,
Wanna play tag?
Though we had the perfect jail space
just two doors down,
I don't think we played Batman
after the summer the Smith's
put a dog pen in their yard.

III

It was made of layers of satin and lace,
supposed to be knee length,
but hit the ground on us.
A treasure for any dress up box,
and I never knew why Diane's sister
gave her a wedding gown to play in.
The fact that it was *ours* and not
a forbidden entity in some closet
did nothing to tarnish its magnificence.
No other kid in school had a real wedding dress.
Of course, I never got to wear it.
Being the youngest,
I got the ratty skirt Mom turned into a
gypsy costume on Halloween,
on the days I was lucky.
Not even a Bridesmaid, just Flower Girl.
On unlucky days, I got jeans and had to be
ring bearer. A boy's job was the worst of the lot.
Diane usually called dibs on the dress
just because it was hers,
but Deb was wearing it the day
the bumblebee showed up.
It flew up between the lace and satin

while Deb screamed and cried and twirled,
yelled at us to get that dress off her.
But we didn't want to get stung by a bumblebee
so we just stood there
wide-eyed in horror

as the bee got caught in the lace
and Deb yelled and cried.
Diane's mom came running onto the porch.
Once they got the dress off,
we all stomped all over it,
then wadded it up, tossed it back in the trunk,
slammed the lid
to keep the bee from getting back out.
It was weeks before we opened it again.
The bee was still stuck in the dress...
death didn't diminish its malevolence in our minds.
But it WAS a wedding dress,
even with shoe prints all over the lace,
and, finally, I could be the bride.
I slipped it over my head,
keeping the bee carcass far from my skin,
pulled up the zipper and turned...
Deb and Diane were pulling
old bathing suit tops from the trunk;
they threw them in the air, calling,
Burn your bras! Liberate women!
I sat down on the step and sighed.

VICTORIA STERLING

Complex

Fingers wrap around my wrist
Measuring my density
Figures flash across the scale
Measuring small victory

I track my progress
First by fractions
Then by inches
Then by days
By weeks, by months
I know the wait will one day do me in

Carefully, I weigh my options
In each hand like justice
In each hand I hold a half-cup
Waver back and forth until
I no longer look for sustenance
I look for meaning

Fingers dig into my body
Hoping I can find the answer
Hoping I can see the reason
Hoping I can feel the bones

Carelessly, I move the goal post
First by inches
Then by miles

I know the weight
Will one day
Do me in

She is Beautiful

It's hard to keep a perfect manicure
When she's clawing her way up a cliff face

It's hard to keep her hair from getting messy
When she's running cross-country
And running the world

She isn't shaped by shapewear
But by years of education

And her make-up isn't merely
Peacock feathers—
It is war paint

What Lies Ahead

Your fear is that your story will be written
In your skin with scalpels and stitches,
And that no one will know your history
When you don't know the future of your body.

Everything will be okay, you hear them say...
And you suppress the urge to shred yourself
And render them wrong.

It hurts when the only direction you're given
Is in books with empty pages
And platitudes with empty promises...

But I find my direction in the corners of your mouth.
Where they go, I will follow,
And my soul will fill the spaces where my body is not able.

HOLLY DAY

The Soldier

I'm standing right behind her in line and I can't help but pass
    judgment, I am not
a good feminist, a good woman, I would be a terrible friend to
    this woman standing here
holding a car seat with a tiny baby in it, a little blond toddler
    clutching her other friend
this woman in combat fatigues buying cases of infant formula
and several months' worth of breakfast cereal and assorted
    dried goods.
Next to her is a man with a beard typing something into his
    phone,
distractedly looking up when the cashier announces the
    grocery total,
looking back down again as the woman pulls out her wallet.

I remember how hard it was to leave my own baby behind
while I worked various temp jobs, my then-husband left in
    charge of our tiny baby
calling home two or three times a day to make sure
my son was all right, ask how many diapers he'd gone through
how many bottles he'd emptied. I can't imagine what it would
    be like
to be deployed so far away from home
that only one phone call a day would be allowed to catch up
    on everything
or none at all for weeks, what it would be like to leave those
    beautiful babies behind
pushed along through every day buoyed only by faith.

Dying on a Monday

I feel her growing quieter beneath the pressure of my hands
flops and flutters like a butterfly drenched in oil, only a few
    moments more
and there will be no more cheerleader left to tell you how
    wonderful you are.

I come upstairs and tell him that I've killed the cheerleader,
    that she's all gone
there will be no more pom pom parades every time he does
    something
mildly intelligent or innovative. He stares at me blankly until
    I explain
there was a cheerleader inside me this whole time, that what
    he's been seeing
is the cheerleader, but now she's gone and there will be no more

twirling flaming batons or happy puppy antics
every time he walks in the door on time, or actually remembers
to pick up milk
or offers an actual compliment instead of some snort of
    derision
at my choice of clothes or shoes or makeup or hairstyle
I have given up on organizing parades or circuses or
    celebrations at the price of dignity
all that is left is me.

Talking it Out

She keeps talking about running away, say it's too much
this isn't her country anymore, this isn't her home.
Fuck sticking it out, she says, being real patriots, standing by our motherland
waiting for things to be normal once more.

We wait her speech out until it's run its course, gently remind her
that there are too many people she'd have to bring along, we make a list.
She'd run over the border dragging an entire city's worth
of relatives and friends, decent neighbors and even a few
well-intentioned people opposed to her particular point of view
not aware of the danger. She'd at least have to bring us.
I pretend to call my son and tell him to get a passport
get it quick, get ready to run, tell him about what happens
to young men when there's a war coming,
tell him his sister's in charge of travel plans.

These are improbable situations. Where would she put the dog, for one thing?
Who would take the cat? Would she rather live where it's violent and warm
or peaceful and cold? Which border to head towards, the closest one
the farthest one? Should we all just get on a plane, leave the continent altogether
is anywhere really safe? How much is all of this
going to cost?

CARRIE GREENLAW

Goddamn Hurricane

I hurled myself into this world
like a hurricane,
clutching ten knives
with a thousand hornets
buzzing through my hair.

I was born on this hill.
I bloomed from the sky
upside down krishna jesus
heysoos and hosannas.
I run this shit.
My veins are thick with red brick
and broken cars and city steps
spanning eighteen trash bags
worth of evictions
and I ain't done yet.

They try to kill me
but I keep coming back,
alleycat coordination
birthday candles
snuffed out in a smack of sulfur
and a deathwish.
They pulled me out from under a car,
two loose teeth and still biting.
They pried me out from under his body,

life gone from our eyes and
I came back whooping like a cowboy,
cracking the hands that held me
and breathing fire in the parking lot.

You can't tame me.

I'm no drugstore pigeon
sadsack puppy rope-tied
to a rain gutter.
I have the heart of a panther
wild and beating double-time
to feed this ruby blood to my limbs,
so I feed my ruby blood what it wants.

When a shark stops swimming he starts dying;
I could walk all the way to Ohio with this baby on my hip.

So get your ass off my porch,
go lock the windows
and cover them with bedsheets,
bleached-out pattern
of flowers and period blood.
Sell the damn car
or drive it off a cliff
to smash onto the highway,
smash the oblivious skulls
lined up like shooting gallery ducks
and air-rifle stars below.

Cause I'm pounding gasoline
and budweiser and headaches
and I'm wounded and hobbled
but never humbled.
My eyes shine as green
as the day I was born
and I'm standing on the tallest
gravestone in the cemetery,
hollering into the eye
of my personal storm
until I can't hear an echo.

Big Bang

I'm a zygote in search of the big bang;
please don't leave me hanging.

The galaxy consumes sheaves of planets
and grows thin,
expanding into cold remoteness.
I'm spread thin over the plate of sky

and all i want
is to replay
the smash at the beginning
when the starfields cracked open
and everyone came
at the same time
without lying.

I squat on my rock and squint, moon-eyed.
Primitive medicine can heal by subtraction -
I pray to the god of knives and feet and scabs.
Melt my bones in a crucible.

There is the cold contraction.
Here is the expansion, viscous
as warm spit in the palm of your hand.

The Summer Room

We press against the suntilt evening,
carving out a private room
atop the daily rot of a felled tree
to stroke hands and sigh.
In haloed sunset,
young couples swarm the train trestle
like ants, kissing through the rust-gold holes.

I remember being young I say,
as if to be young is to be foolish
but here I am, limp-necked and nervous,
swanning under an armpit.

Last spring a tent appeared
beside the switchyard and slowly
the clearing turned candyland:
dumpstered garden ringing the pissbucket
and two bicycles chained
together, like yoked oxen.

The height of summer brought a thunderclap disarray
and cardboard, sharpie-stabbed *already robbed,
nothing left to steal*
and soon they were gone,
a square dirt footprint
dissolving like aspirin.

Who termites the stoop
of the river now?
Who will be there to hear
the rat scatter of evening
in the room we pressed
into the warm palm of summer?

I walk into the night alone.
I walk into my house on the hill alone.
The honey locust presses
the memory of leaves
skyward.

LINDA LERNER

When Death Is a Red Balloon

Scared shitless last week when I
came to your room, saw you asleep
and kept calling your name
pulling your hand, *wake up*, I shouted
until you opened your eyes…

Oh, I tried again, sat by your bed for hours
holding your hand, sending my voice like a rope
to where you lay several levels below sleep

love, which never made it into word,
flowed through my touch with the meds from IV's
that kept you breathing

and then I saw that red balloon
like those in comics, instead of words,
a wire scrawl of hieroglyphics,
once there, wouldn't go away

I didn't want to see it hovering
near you, but I did; how you'd hate it,
It's not funny, you'd say, blaming me
for what I couldn't control

I watched the air slowly being let out.
Three hours passed and I left…it was just before…

the balloon is gone now
you are asleep, I am by your bedside
once again, holding your hand

if you can hear me, I must tell you
there is nothing I can ever imagine experiencing
more horrible than watching the air go out
of that balloon

Keeping Time

He had three other watches ticking off
his remaining time to remind him
but it's that watch I like to think of
keeping time in one of those jewelry stores
in Manhattan's west 40's, a Rolex
maybe Longenes, ticking, like a heart
beating up to its last breath
ticket lost and he couldn't recall exactly where
kept good time, his heart beating strong,
the band stretched to its limits
his body headed in reverse, a '59 white convertible Ford
he could no longer drive speeding
back to 1980's *The Real Thing* we shared
through March 2016, the curtain
coming down on O'Neil's Hughie.

Like A Prayer

Something about his, *I like your shoes*
after I read something sad
because that's the way it's been since
it will get easier, words last July
struck me as funny, and why today,
not quite a year later, grateful that
no one had used the word, closure,
I even wore those red beaded moccasins
which had no support, weren't comfortable
thank you, I said to this man I barely knew
trying hard to suppress a laugh
I couldn't hold back any longer
as more and more people began to stare
at my shoes and I slipped away
whispering, thank you,
like a prayer

TOBI ALFIER

High Tea
For Amy

Shoulders and biceps tough,
shapely as a wrought iron
balustrade on a Bourbon Street
balcony, from thousands
of pushups in 5:00am PT,
flushed face a match for the rise
of dawn, always the count
inside her head—*forty, fifty,
sixty*, controlled face lowered
onto cool grass.

Now she is at tea,
a *Breakfast at Tiffany's* frock,
off the shoulder, over the knee,
I am a lovely woman she thinks,
her reflection poised in the many mirrors.
Legs crossed, patent-leather pumps,
tiny earrings peep through hair
delicately placed over her ears.
A pot of Earl Grey at her elbow,
sweets and sandwiches to the side.

No stripes, no boots, no salutes.
This is a day to remember the quiet
goodness of daily blessings, the definition
of friend. This man—this gentleman—

who doesn't keep score, or harbor resentment
like a plague…She could get a PhD
in disappointment, but no fieldwork
will be done today. The only decisions—
wildflower honey or acacia, and which flowers
to bring home to grace both their houses.

The Scent of New-Mown Wildflowers

A day where she wakes with a calm smile,
the sound of the chime at the front door
means only one thing—confirmed by the melody
of rain on the bricks outside. Straight down rain,
like the sound of slowly poured brandy
from a crystal decanter into a tilted glass.

She burrows under quilts, always white,
provenances from different years,
different explorations. He stands under the eaves
on the porch, hand outstretched, eyes closed
as drops read his palm, the just-gone-spring
fortune teller with water rather than tarot.

They went to sleep last night with wind
banging their small boat against their small dock
both treasure and trial for river-living.
Never the bright perfume of blackened waves,
but the ocean was not their sacred place,
their grasses-to-the-water's-edge place,

their we-don't-speak-this-language
but together we can translate, and lanterns
are right outside just in case place.
She can hear the early-service choir
from the raised church across the water—
five wooden steps up to keep out floods

and snakes, tall weed-flowers growing
up on either side, all of it canted
a bit to the left—like everyone living
in this village-town of saints and wanderers.
Here they will be married, in time, in time,
blessed by the midday radiance of true summer.

Hymn of the Farmer's Daughter

Wind carries the perfume of lavender
over sun-saturated green and bright fields
of the south, where she walks barefoot
and dancing, sundress blown sideways
by gusts of breeze, drafted by trucks
doing eighty on the flat strip of highway
that breaks the ground between blossom
and flock. Many a farmer owns both.
Many a farmer's daughter is just like her:

sandals swing from one hand, other hand holds
a length of hair behind one ear. Songs from the radio
hummed under her breath happily, make dimples
deeper. No watch. No purse. A tenner
tucked inside her waist in case thirst
don't make it back home—in case
the violinist who busks on the corner of Middle
and Main is there, his pride written off
to loss, sweet sadness in his melodies,
his case open for anything given—
for a sandwich now, a bourbon later, a room
for the night even later still.

Railcars screech way yonder, mark the boundary
of this farmer's land. She has barely been farther
than that, and that's okay with her. She recalls
watching her parents slow-dance in the kitchen
on the chipped linoleum. Not bravery. Not cowardice.

She wants the same for herself. Her wish to wrap arms
'round the broken busker, bring him home to solitude,
a place she knows the wind carries no voices,
where he'll write songs just for her,
slow-dance in the kitchen just with her—
footsteps moving with vagrant grace.

DAWN CLAYTON

The Key

A key is not just to open something
It's to lock things up good and tight
And when you lose a key it's a big deal
I have a drawer in me
with good things inside
But it's locked tight and
I can't find the key
I have keys but none will work
Maybe you have the key
To unlock the joy inside of me

Dirty Kids

Dirty kids on concrete beds
Holding on to metal blankets
Brown kids
Not white kids
5 month old kids
17 year old kids
9 year old kids
And all in between
Where is that worthless mom
Where is that worthless dad
Deported you say
Kids left behind you say
No, kids kept behind
Kids kept behind in abusive conditions
Imposed by the leader of the home of the brave
and land of the free
Where are the brave

Where Does He Go?

Where does he go behind those eyes
A place I can not go
A place he will not let me go
He leaves for hours in the woods
A place he will not let me go
when this domestic scene is too much for him
He does not trust me or anyone
His walls are high and thick
Forty years by his side and I get a glimpse
but only when he opens up
to others of shared experience
I will continue to love him
One day he may let me go where he goes

DENISE TERRIAH

Good Boy

Maybe if I'd been paying attention there wouldn't be so much blood now. I watched it idly as it soaked into the knees of my stockings. I should have been scared, or sad, but all I felt was relieved. Good boy.

Obviously, this story didn't start on my knees in a pool of blood. It started because the dog was as black as the night around me and I didn't see it before it was in the headlights. I slammed the brake pedal to the floor and the tires locked up obediently sending me skidding across the wet pavement. Jeff was still on the phone that I'd dropped into my lap so I could grab the wheel with both hands. His voice was a buzzing muffled by my skirt that I didn't notice until the car had come to a stop after a loud thump. I sat briefly panting in the glow of the dash lights before I realized I should back my car off the road which was just an empty, lightless, ribbon stretched out in the darkness between two towns.

"What the hell was that?" Jeff demanded when I lifted the phone back to my ear, never taking my eyes off the side of the road, where I was straining to distinguish one dark shape from the rest of the night.

"I think I hit a dog."

"Dammit Alice. What do ya mean ya hit a dog? Weren't ya looking at the road? Jeezus, so help me, if you messed up the car I'm going to take the cost out of your hide."

I let out the breath I'd been holding, "I'll pay for it. I swear."

You're damn right you're going to pay for it. Now get your ass home or I'm gonna come find you." He hung up abruptly leaving the threat hanging in the air.

    I stared at the phone in my hand for a moment before dropping it into my purse and opening the door of the car. My foot nearly slipped out from under me as I stepped out. It wasn't until I gripped the door tightly to regain my footing that I noticed my arms and legs were trembling. Was it because I was afraid of what I would see, or that I still had to go home after?

    When I stepped around the fender I could see the dark shape on the side of the road. The force of the impact had thrown it off into the weeds. The light was dimmer than it should have been so I stumbled over shadows in my haste to reach the poor creature. Looking back at the car it was clear one of my headlights was dark, probably broken. I winced. I didn't know how much it would cost in dollars, but I could guess what it was going to cost in punishment.

    I turned my attention back to the animal in front of me. It had to be dead didn't it? The fur was so dark it looked like a liquid shadow. I put my hand on its body, the chest rose and fell slowly. At least it was alive. The fur was damp, but so hot I pulled my fingers back. It was unnerving. The dog smelled like smoke, like it had rolled in the cinders of a fire to obtain its color. I studied my fingers in the dim light. They were clean other than a light sheen of water but
I couldn't resist the urge to wipe them off on my thigh.

    Part of me wanted to run back to the car and not look back, but I couldn't just leave the animal like this. Instead, I slipped my arms under it and struggled to cradle the dog to my body. It wasn't a small dog to begin with, but it was a lot heavier than it looked. When I had it settled in the back seat, I started the engine and turned the car around.

✶

"Where the hell are ya?"

I squeezed my eyes shut and chewed on my lower lip. "I'm at Parkway Animal Hospital."

The phone sat ominously quiet. After a space of silence long enough that I wondered if the call had dropped, Jeff spoke. "Who exactly is gonna pay for that?" His voice was calm and controlled in a way that scared me more than when he yelled.

"I will of course."

"So now your job pays well enough to cover damages to the car and an animal hospital?"

"I can get some overtime…" I started.

"Overtime she says. So, with this overtime you can still get your chores done and dinner on the table?" Jeff interrupted before I could finish my sentence. "Speaking of which, it's dinner time now, and do you know what I'm eating?"

"One night…"

"No Alice, that's not how this works. I'm eating nothing right now. You'd better not make this a habit, because that would make me mad."

"Excuse me Miss." The man who'd spoken was standing in front of me wearing green scrubs with little, rainbow-colored, paw prints all over them.

"I have to go, the vet's here," I mumbled hastily into the phone.

"Don't you hang up on …" I tapped the red icon and put the phone back in my purse. I was going to have a lot to answer for tonight, but I didn't want to leave the vet waiting.

"Are you the young woman who thought she hit the black dog?"

The man's smile was friendly, but I nodded while my cheeks burned. I felt terrible.

"He's fine. No broken bones. Doesn't seem to be in any pain. He woke up a couple of minutes ago. Are you sure you hit him? Is it possible you hit a rock or something?"

"I guess it's possible," I answered while shaking my head, I didn't want to argue with the vet, but I hadn't hit a rock.

"You said he's not your dog, but he doesn't have a collar. We scanned him; he doesn't have a chip either. Do you want to take him home with you, or are you going to turn him in to the shelter we're affiliated with?"

An assistant in bright orange scrubs with dogs printed on them led the black dog down the hall on a leash. He looked even bigger standing up, magnified, imposing. His muzzle was set in an unfriendly line and his eyes looked fierce. I frowned. I wasn't sure why my brain chose those words because he was also shaggy, and perfectly calm.

I wanted to say yes to leaving him at the shelter. He made the back of my neck prickle, but his eyes were an accusation and I felt guiltier looking into them then I had thus far. I hadn't meant to do it, but I found myself holding my hand out for the leash.

I'd dug my credit card out at the front desk feeling numb while the dog stood quietly next to me. He could have nearly rested his head on my hip if he'd wanted. Was he bigger than when I carried him to the car?

The entire ride home I could smell the stench of smoke on the dog's fur. I'd tried to put him in the back seat, but he'd climbed calmly into the passenger seat and stared at me as if daring me to tell him otherwise. He never made a sound, but he had a calm, heavy energy that made me want to move away from him. That was unfortunately impossible in the car.

"Come on buddy, we're here." The dog waited

patiently until I opened the door then he gingerly stepped out of the car. Jeff was going to freak out when I walked in there, but with a dog in tow he was liable to go through the roof. I shouldn't have brought him home, but I owed the dog something. I'd hit him with a car, no matter what the vet said, I knew I'd hit him.

I'd barely started to put my key in the door when it was flung open, ripping the knob out of my hand.

"Well look who finally decided to come home." Jeff leaned in and I could smell the whiskey on his breath. I took a deep breath, there'd be no avoiding it tonight.

"I thought I was going to have to go looking for you," he smiled grabbing my wrist and squeezing until it felt like he was trying to smash one bone using the other.

"I'm sorry." It was barely a whisper. I didn't dare raise my voice. I didn't want to make this worse than it was already going to be.

"You're right, you're the sorriest ass I've ever seen."

He jerked my arm sharply downward as he dragged me through the door. I stumbled to my knees in front of him. The first blow took me on the side of the face. It was open-handed, but that didn't mean it didn't hurt. Spots swam in my vision and I could taste blood. Jeff's hand wrapped into my hair as he pulled my face upward. I had my eyes squeezed shut. I didn't want to see the next blow coming. It was almost better if I didn't brace for it. I gasped several ragged breaths but the blow didn't come, and his hand eased slowly out of my hair, like he'd had a change of heart. That wasn't like him at all.

When I opened my eyes, I didn't know what I was seeing. I briefly worried that the first blow had done more damage than I realized. Jeff stood perfectly still, his eyes wide, a rivulet of blood dribbled from the corner of his mouth. Below that, what looked like four black spikes protruded from the front of his neck, and I could smell meat burning. Behind him a shape I couldn't make sense of appeared to glow from the inside, casting dark shadows around it like a flickering fire burned within it, but the skin was still inky black. It was emitting light without being illuminated itself. Before the initial horror of the figure could sink in the four spikes pulled backwards through the flesh of Jeff's neck and blood spurted from the wounds.

    His body slipped to the floor. No, that wasn't the right word, it crumpled, like the spikes had been holding him upright. Without Jeff in between us I was staring straight at the creature. It was human-shaped without looking human. Nobody would ever mistake this for a human.

    It bent down and its darkness flowed over Jeff's twitching limbs like a blanket, until the darkness was shapeless, and no longer inhumanly human. There was a sound unlike anything I'd ever heard. It was like a groaning that echoed with thousands of shrieks in some far-off distant place. I didn't realize I'd stopped breathing until my lungs ached with the need for air. As I gasped, the edges of the thing in front of me went wavy, like the surface of water, and coalesced into the dog. I'd forgotten him on the front step. Jeff's body was simply gone. The beast in front of me watched me with its hard eyes and its tail wagged briefly. Then it bent to the blood that was oozing across the floor in a slow puddle, and began to lap it up.

    I hugged myself as I kneeled on the floor. I should have been afraid. I probably should have run away. Instead I watched the black dog licking up the blood. It wasn't paying any attention to me. He might still kill me too, but right now all that mattered was that I was finally free.

TERESA COSTA

Summer Queen

Queen Anne's Lace, ruled over the wild Daisies
That summer. Queen of the roadside along w/
The overcrowding of purplish blue Chicory.
Milkweed had moved too far out into roadside,
Where Monarchs wood feed/feel the poison of
Motorized vehicles, exhaust, oil & gasoline.
The rains outdid Tiger/Daylilies. Practically
Stunted in growth, just short of drowning.
Worms, Millipedes celebrated the dampness.
Some held nightly festivities, while the Ants those
Socialized pests tried vainly to overtake my
Household.

Glowed In The Dark

We saved the juice of Fireflies
Drank it under the blankets
Hoping we'd glow at night

With Black Elk

Yr death over-shadows the tail end
Of a moon new for this month of August.
62 years past & 5 before my incarnated birth.
We were classmates & teachers,
 In that last single dimension.
As our souls made one last decision.
You stayed behind enjoying life w/o pain
	w/o feeling
	w/o affliction.
I kept on moving through the stages,
got reborn.
Reincarnated to a new world of pain
	& feeling.
Only my world is now w/o
the headdress of turkey feathers

The Players:

Tobi Alfier is a multiple Pushcart nominee and multiple Best of the Net nominee. Her full-length collection *Somewhere, Anywhere, Doesn't Matter Where* was published by Kelsay Books. *Slices of Alice & Other Character Studies* was published by Cholla Needles Press. *Sanity Among the Wildflowers,* her very first chapbook (2005) was just reprinted by Cholla Needles Press. She is co-editor of *San Pedro River Review* (www.bluehorsepress.com).

Nikki Allen is a lover & a writer—with hair an animal & heart clumsy tiger. Scribbling because she must with nearly 20 years of stages in her gut. She has read in cities across the US at music festivals, war protests, backyards and art openings. She is the author of numerous books, including *Gutter of Eden, Quite Like Yes,* and *Ligaments of Light/Tigering the Shoulders* (Night Ballet Press). Her work has appeared in *Nailed, Crash, The New Yinzer, out of nothing, Profane Journal*(Pushcart Prize nominee '14/'15) and *Encyclopedia Destructica* among others. Allen has also contributed vocals to tracks by recording artists Poogie Bell (Question Song) and Jack Wilson (NYC). She believes in revolution, strong coffee, the hard knocks & the sweetness.

Jyl Anais is a poet and visual artist working at the intersections of a variety of media. She has worked as an advocate for victims of child abuse in the court system, as well as with law enforcement and in the private sector as a forensic medium. Originally from Trinidad, Jyl now lives in the United States where she nurtures orchids and faces the blank page. Soft Out Spoken, her first collection of poems, will be available in stores soon. Find her at jylanais.com.

Stephanie Bryant Anderson earned her B.S. in English and Psychology from Austin Peay State University. Her poems have appeared or are forthcoming in *The Normal School, Passages North, Underblong, Mid-American Review* and others. Currently Stephanie is completing an M.S. in Mental Health Counseling.

Claudia Bierschenk's poetry has been published in *Juice Press, Full of Crow, Alittlepoetry, Durable Goods, SAND Journal, Alligator Stew, Hanzir, Tangerine Press,* and in several print prose and poetry anthologies by Pure Slush. Her first poetry chapbook *Perestroika Silence* was published by erbacce Press, Liverpool in 2010. Her second chapbook *Luther* was published by PigEar Press, UK, 2017. Claudia lives in Berlin with her son.

Dianne Borsenik, poet, performer, producer, and publisher, is active in the northern Ohio poetry scene and regional reading circuit. She is a former flowerchild and current redhead. She lives in a temple of happiness with her husband James.

D.C. Buschmann is a retired editor and reading specialist. Her poem, *Death Comes for a Friend,* was the Editor's Choice in *Poetry Quarterly,* Winter 2018. She has been a finalist in several essay and poetry contests. Her work appears in anthologies in the US, the UK, Australia, Iraq, and India and has been in or will appear in Kurt Vonnegut Museum and Library's *So it Goes Literary Journal, Flying Island, The Adirondack Review, San Pedro River Review, The Great American Wise Ass* by Lamar University Press, *Rat's Ass Review, Nerve Cowboy,* and elsewhere. Her first book of poems is in the pondered stage.

Dawn Clayton is an attorney and longtime resident of Vienna, Missouri.

Teresa Costa has been writing, reading, performing her poetry since 1974. Thanks in part to the late jazz poet; Ray Bremser & minor beat poet; George Montgomery. Costa's poems have been published in *Home Planet News, The Chronogram, A Slant of Light - Codhill press, Stained Sheets, The Woodstock Times, Up The River Journal,* amongst many others. Currently hosts Word oF Mouth Poetry Series in Kingston, NY USA.

Nancy Patrice Davenport is a native of the San Francisco Bay Area and lives in Sonora, California. Her poems are widely published in various journals and anthologies, and have been translated into many languages. Nancy's *June 2 Retrograde Mindfulness* poem was nominated for the 2016 Best of Net. Her first chapbook, *La Brizna*, was published in 2014 by Bookgirl Press. A full-length book of poems, *Smoking In Mom's Garage,* was published in 2018 by Red Alice Press.

Holly Day has taught writing classes at the Loft Literary Center in Minneapolis, Minnesota, since 2000. Her poetry has recently appeared in *Tampa Review, SLAB,* and *Gargoyle.*

Trina L. Drotar writes poetry, fiction, nonfiction, poetry, screenplays, and she is a visual artist working with fiber, ink, printmaking, collage, mixed media, watercolor, and photography. She's received numerous awards across all literary and visual arts categories. Her latest projects The Blue Shirt, Return to Bialowieza, and Alice Ventures Into the Night Garden. She has been widely published and recorded, and her artwork is held in several public and private collections. She teaches workshops, writes journalism and book reviews, judges exhibits, edits and coaches, lifts weights, reads daily, and loves her cats. She may be reached at TrinaLDrotar@gmail.com.

Alexis Rhone Fancher is published in *Best American Poetry, Verse Daily, Plume, The American Journal of Poetry, Rattle, Hobart, Diode, Nashville Review, Wide Awake, Poets of Los Angeles, Rust + Moth, Cleaver, Slipstream,* and elsewhere. She's the author of 5 poetry collections; *How I Lost My Virginity To Michael Cohen,* (2014), *State of Grace: The Joshua Elegies,* (2015), *Enter Here,* (2017), *Junkie Wife,* (2018), and *The Dead Kid Poems* (2019). *EROTIC, New & Selected,* publishes in 2020 from New York Quarterly. A multiple Pushcart Prize and Best of the Net nominee, Alexis is poetry editor of *Cultural Weekly.* www.alexisrhonefancher.com

Sandra Feen is the Speak No Evil Monkey in the poetry troupe Concrete Wink, with Chuck Salmons and Rikki Santer. Her most recent publications include her book *Meat and Bone* (Luchador Press 2019), and work in *The National Beat Poetry Foundation, Inc. We Are Beat* (2019) and *The Gasconade Review's Storm A' Comin'!* (2019) anthologies. Her book *Fragile Capacities: School Poems* (NightBallet Press 2018) – nominated for the Ohioana Book Award – highlights her 32-year teaching career in an urban school system. The poem "Palms Monday" was nominated for a Pushcart Prize. More of her work is forthcoming in *The Gasconade Review's Ladies' Night* (2019).

Robin Freeland is a private music instructor who lives in Jefferson City, Missouri. She volunteered for several years in the JCHE Homeschool Organization, helping to facilitate Speech and Debate Tournaments in many key roles. Judging these events also assisted her in developing a subconscious cranial compartment of valuable memories that trickle through to the prefrontal cortex, illuminating her imagination.

Carrie Greenlaw is a poet and artist from the North Side of Pittsburgh. Her work has been featured in *The Pittsburgh Poetry Review, River* and *South Review, Masque & Spectacle* and *Inscape Magazine*. Her debut chapbook, *Dark Garnet,* was published by L&S Press as the 2019 selection for their Mid-Atlantic Chapbook Series. Carrie lives low and lives slow.

A. Summer Javadi was raised in Rich Hill, Missouri; but, has lived most of her life in the Kansas City, Missouri metropolitan area. Javadi received first prize publishing in the 2018 Spring edition of *Inferno Literary Magazine* for her poem, *If Guns Were Made of Crayons*. Summer is the mother of five beautiful children and wife of Rabbi Mort where she mutually teaches Hebraic studies for their non for profit; Mahi Ministries Inc.

Kyle Laws is based out of the Arts Alliance Studios Community in Pueblo, CO where she directs Line/Circle: Women Poets in Performance. Her collections include *Ride the Pink Horse* (Stubborn Mule Press), *Faces of Fishing Creek* (Middle Creek Publishing), *So Bright to Blind* (Five Oaks Press), and *Wildwood* (Lummox Press). With six nominations for a Pushcart Prize, her poems and essays have appeared in magazines and anthologies in the U.S., U.K., Canada, and France. She is the editor and publisher of Casa de Cinco Hermanas Press.

Linda Lerner's latest poetry collection, *A Dance Around the Cauldron,* is a prose work consisting of nine characters during the Salem witch trials brought into our own times (Lummox Press, 2017. Previously published books: *Yes, the Ducks Were*

Real & Takes Guts and *Years Sometimes* (NYQ Books (2011 & 2015). *When Death is a Red Balloon,* a chapbook of poems will be published by Lummox Press in 2019; "Taking the F Train" was accepted by NYQ Books.

Karen Lillis is the author of four novellas, including *Watch the Doors as They Close* (Spuyten Duyvil). Her writing (fiction, poetry, memoir essays) has appeared in such publications as *The Brooklyn Rail, Cabildo Quarterly, Composite Arts Magazine, Evergreen Review, LA Cultural Weekly, LitHub, Local Knowledge, Potomac Journal, TRIPcity,* and *Volume 1 Brooklyn,* among others. She was a regular contributor to *New York Nights,* a newspaper of poetry and anti-war sentiment that emerged after September 11. Her books of fiction earned her a 2014 Acker Award for Avant-Garde Excellence and her article about the small presses of Pittsburgh landed her a finalist position for a Western Pennsylvania journalism award, The Golden Quill.

Ellaraine Lockie is widely published and awarded as a poet, nonfiction book author and essayist. Her fourteenth chapbook, *Sex and Other Slapsticks,* was recently released from Presa Press. Earlier collections have won *Poetry Forum's* Chapbook Contest Prize, San Gabriel Valley Poetry Festival Chapbook Competition, Encircle Publications Chapbook Contest, Best Individual Poetry Collection Award from *Purple Patch magazine* in England, and The Aurorean's Chapbook Choice Award. She also teaches writing workshops and serves as Poetry Editor for the lifestyles magazine, *LILIPOH*.

Pegarty Long was born in New York City, New York, USA. She is a producer and director, known for *An Irish Vampire in Hollywood* (AKA *'The Irish Vampire Goes West).*

Laura Martin is a free-lance writer and photographer whose work has appeared in publications throughout California including: *Tule Review, Late Peaches: Poems by Sacramento Poets, Medusa's Kitchen, Convergence – An Online Journal of Poetry and Art, Sacramento Voices, Verse on the Vine, Susurrus* and *Soul of the Narrator*. Her poetry has been nominated for a Pushcart Prize and has won the grand prize in the Second Annual Pat Schneider Poetry Contest. Martin fronts The Soft Offs – a spoken word/ jazz/ blues/ beer band that takes the written word from page to stage.

Jonie McIntire is the author of *Beyond the Sidewalk* (NightBallet Press, 2017) and *Not All Who Are Lost Wander* (Finishing Line Press, 2016) and her upcoming chapbook *Semidomesticated* will be released by Nightballet Press in 2020. She hosts two monthly poetry reading series in Toledo, Ohio and is poetry editor for *Springboard*, a teen literary journal. Recipient of an Arts Commission Accelerator Grant, she has poems published in journals across the country and even stamped into cement in Toledo as part of the Arts Commission's Sidewalk Poetry series.

Barbara Marie Minney writes personal and emotional poetry that describes her feelings, thoughts, and passions while struggling to live her truth as a transgender woman. She began her transition to living authentically as the woman that she now knows she was meant to be a little over two years ago at the age of 63 after repressing her true gender identity for over 60 years. Barbara serves as a member of the Board of Directors of the Community Aids Network/Akron Pride Initiative (CANAPI).

April Pameticky is a mother of two, and shares time between her high school English classroom and the creative community of artists and writers in Kansas. She launched the Wichita Broadside Project 2017 and currently serves as editor of *River City Poetry.*

Puma Perl is a writer and the author of four solo poetry collections; a fifth will be published by Beyond Baroque Press, 2019. Since 2012, she's presented *Puma Perl's Pandemonium*, which merges spoken word with rock and roll, and she performs regularly her band. She's received three awards from the New York Press Association in recognition of her journalism as well as the 2016 Acker Award in the category of writing. She is a lifelong NYC resident.

Wendy Rainey's latest book, *Girl On The Highway* was published by Picture Show Press in 2019. She is a contributing poetry editor on Chiron Review. Her poetry has appeared in *Nerve Cowboy, Trailer Park Quarterly, Red Fez, Hobo Camp Review,* and *Chiron Review* among others.

Rikki Santer's work has appeared in various publications including *Ms. Magazine, Poetry East, Margie, Hotel Amerika, The American Journal of Poetry, Slab, Crab Orchard Review, RHINO, Grimm, Slipstream, Midwest Review* and *The Main Street Rag*. My seventh poetry collection, *In Pearl Broth*, was just published by Stubborn Mule Press.

Lauren Scharhag is a multi-genre author and poet. Her titles include *Requiem for a Robot Dog* (Cajun Mutt Press), *West Side Girl & Other Poems, The Order of the Four Sons series* (with Coyote Kishpaugh), *The Ice Dragon, The Winter Prince,*

Under Julia, and *Our Miss Engel*. Her work has appeared in over 100 literary venues around the world. She is the recipient of the Door is a Jar Award and the Gerard Manley Hopkins Award for poetry, as well as a fellowship from Rockhurst University for fiction. She lives in Kansas City, MO. To learn more about her work, visit: www.laurenscharhag.blogspot.com

Maureen Sherbondy's work has appeared in *Calyx, Feminist Studies, European Judaism*, and other journals. She teaches English at Alamance Community College in Graham, North Carolina. and lives in Durham.

Marcy Smalley, Composer, visual artist and retired urban planner.

Victoria Sterling lives in Jefferson City, MO with her husband, J. Mat Kendrick. Her writing is inspired by social and political struggles and the efforts of the people around her who wish to make the world a better place. She enjoys a glass of wine and a good portmanteau.

Trins Stolec and her black cat, Icabod, travel the Realm of The Muse conjuring poetry and allowing it to escape into the Collective Cosmos. A party often ensues since the pair is always accompanied by at least one of Trina's many personalities. On occasion, they pick up a musician and, under the moniker of Logic Alley, the Intrepid Duo takes on the fight for Truth, Justice, and The American Way (non-revised edition) on stages across the area. At other times, Trina puts her acting training to work and pretends to be a normal person.

Michelle Storer Michelle Storer lives in Coventry, England. She loves nineties indie rock and Siamese cats. Her work has featured in *Storm a 'Comin – The Gasconade Review*

Presents Paperback (May 2019), *Scare Devil* – A chapbook journal of new poetry published by Tangerine Press (April 2019), *Poetry Card Series 8* by Holy & Intoxicated Press (Jan 2019) and also as *Chapbook No 9* - part of Concrete Meat Press' Solid Flesh for Food series (2017)

Heather Sullivan's work has appeared in numerous online and print journals and is forthcoming in *Chiron Review* and *Iniquity Press*. She is the co-editor of *Live Nude Poem*s online and her most recent poetry collection, *Method Acting for the Afterlife,* was released from Nixes Mate Books this year.

Denise Terriah lives in Missouri with her husband and two daughters. She works on her hobby farm by day, attempts to sleep by night, and writes by hiding where nobody can find her to ask for snacks. She likes to think of herself as a novelist but, short stories fill her time between long bouts of writer's block. She's the author of the fictional novel, *As It Ends.*

Penny Thieme is a visual artist, poet, curator, collaborator and visionary. Her art has been featured in solo and group exhibitions such as Artists Fight Back Against the War on Women, Garden of Jungian Delights, Oracles & Vessels and Passages. Her artwork has been published, is in national and international private collections and has been featured in Beyond Bounds at The Nerman Museum of Contemporary Art and the prestigious *River Market Regional.*

Agnes Vojta grew up in Germany, spent a few years in California, Oregon, and England, and now lives in Rolla where she teaches physics at Missouri S&T. She is the author of *Porous Land* (Spartan Press, 2019). Her poems recently appeared in *As It Ought To Be Magazine, Gasconade Review, Thimble Literary Magazine, Trailer Park Quarterly, Poetry Quarterly, Sonic Boom*, and elsewhere.

Baroness Von Smith wrote her first story when she was six. Everybody died in the end. It was a comedy. Today, she is a novelist and produced playwright. She currently spends most of her time in Western New York where she shares her home with two cats and one husband. Occasionally, she travels with the cats.

Loretta Diane Walker is a multiple Pushcart and Best of the Net nominee who has published four collections of poetry and her manuscript *Ode to My Mother's Voice and Other Poems* is forthcoming in 2019. Her manuscript In *This House* won the 2016 Phillis Wheatly Award; *Word Ghetto* won the 2011 Bluelight Press Book Award. Loretta received a BME from Texas Tech University, her MA from the University of Texas Permian Basin. She teaches music at Reagan Magnet School in Odessa, Texas.

Francine Witte is the author of four poetry chapbooks, one full-length collection, and the forthcoming, *Theory of Flesh* from Kelsay Books. Her flash fiction has appeared in numerous journals, anthologized in the most recent *New Micro* (W.W. Norton) and her novella-in-flash, *The Way of the Wind* is forthcoming from Ad Hoc Fiction, as well as a full-length collection of flash fiction, *Dressed All Wrong for This* which is forthcoming from Blue Light Press. She lives in New York City, USA.

Beverly Zeimer is of Appalachian descent; whose writing celebrates life in rural Ohio. She is the author of *Pick a Way* (a county in Ohio) published by Pudding House as winner of a Pudding House Chapbook Competition and *The Wildness of Flowers by Night* Ballet Press. She has been published by The Ohio University Shawnee Press, Wooster College, and *The Long*

Islander edited by George Wallace, and other journals. She is working on a full-length collection of poetry and short stories she calls *The Farmer's Daughter*. She shares her work as a featured reader at coffee houses, poetry events, and festivals throughout Ohio. She lives in Southern Ohio by Big Darby Creek where she enjoys the quiet of nature

Ryki Zuckerman is the author of *the gone artists* (Nixes Mate Books, 2019), *the skirt at the center of the universe* (The Writer's Den, 2018), *a bright nowhere* (Foot Hills Publishing, 2015), and *Looking for Bora Bora* (Saddle Road Press, 2013), Three Poems (University of Buffalo Poetry Collection, 2017), Zuckerman is a longtime co-editor of *Earth's Daughters* magazine. Her work has appeared in *Paterson Literary Review, Lips, Black Mountain College II Review, Slipstream, Dispatches from the Poetry Wars,* and *A Celebration of Western New York Poets* (Buffalo Legacy Press, 2015). She holds a Masters in Art Education from SUNY College at Buffalo.

Sensitivity to Initial Conditions by Penny Thieme

This project was made possible, in part, by generous support from the Osage Arts Community.

Osage Arts Community provides temporary time, space and support for the creation of new artistic works in a retreat format, serving creative people of all kinds — visual artists, composers, poets, fiction and nonfiction writers. Located on a 152-acre farm in an isolated rural mountainside setting in Central Missouri and bordered by ¾ of a mile of the Gasconade River, OAC provides residencies to those working alone, as well as welcoming collaborative teams, offering living space and workspace in a country environment to emerging and mid-career artists. For more information, visit us at www.osageac.org

www.ingramcontent.com/pod-product-compliance
Lightning Source LLC
Chambersburg PA
CBHW030108100526
44591CB00009B/335